MW01618537

dedication

It is doubtful whether my venture into Performance Art would have happened were it not for the encouragement and guidance of choreographer Marsha Paludan to whom I dedicate this book.

—Roger Shimomura

For Kim,
who started this —
Roger

masking identity:

The Performance Art of Roger Shimomura

by Krystal Reiko Hauseur

All photographs were taken by and courtesy of Roger Shimomura.

Printed by CreateSpace, an Amazon Company

Graphic Design:
Erin Shigaki/Purple Gate Design and G. Page Tanagi

Publisher's Cataloging-in-Publication Data
Krystal Reiko Hauseur, Ph.D.
Masking Identity: The Performance Art of Roger Shimomura /
Krystal Reiko Hauseur, Ph.D. / Roger Shimomura
ISBN: 0692965491
ISBN 13: 9780692965498
1. Historical — Bibliography. 2. Japanese American.
3. Performance Art. 4. Experimental Theater.

Library of Congress Control Number:
2019905370
Seattle, WA 98122

First Edition
Printed in the United States of America

table of contents

About the Author:

krystal reiko hauseur, ph.d.

Krystal Reiko Hauseur is an independent scholar and curator of Asian American art. She received her Ph.D. in visual studies at the University of California, Irvine, where she focused on combining the fields of art history and ethnic studies.

Some of her most recent projects include "The Crafted Abstraction of Ruth Asawa, Kay Sekimachi, and Toshiko Takaezu," in *American Women Artists, 1935–1970: Gender, Culture, and Politics* (Routledge, 2016); "Sugar/Islands: Finding Okinawa in Hawai'i—the Art of Laura Kina and Emily Hanako Momohara" (Japanese American National Museum, Bear River Press, 2015); "Visual Art" in *Asian American Society: An Encyclopedia* (Sage, 2014); and "Wendy Maruyama: The Tag Project/Executive Order 9066" (San Diego State University, Japanese American Historical Society, San Diego, and *Footprints*, March 2012).

About the Artist:
roger shimomura

Roger Shimomura's paintings, prints, and theatre pieces address sociopolitical issues of ethnicity. He was born in Seattle, Washington and spent two early years of his childhood in Minidoka (Idaho), one of ten concentration camps for Japanese Americans during WWII. Shimomura was a distinguished military graduate (1962) from the University of Washington, Seattle and served as a field artillery officer with the First Cavalry Division in Korea. In 1969 he received his M.F.A. from Syracuse University, New York. Shimomura began teaching at the University of Kansas, Lawrence, Kansas in 1969. He has had over 150 solo exhibitions of paintings and prints, as well as presented his experimental theater pieces at such venues as the Franklin Furnace, New York City, Walker Art Center, Minneapolis, and the Smithsonian Institution, Washington, D.C. He is the recipient of more than thirty grants, of which four are National Endowment for the Arts Fellowships in Painting and Performance Art. In the fall of 1990, Shimomura held an appointment as the Dayton Hudson Distinguished Visiting Professor at Carleton College, Northfield, Minnesota. Shimomura has been a visiting artist and lectured on his work at more than 200 universities, art schools, and museums across the country. In 2002 he received the College Art Association Distinguished Body of Work Award. The following year, he delivered the keynote address at the 91st annual meeting of CAA in New York City. In 2003 he was a recipient of the Joan Mitchell Foundation Painting Award. In 2006 he was accorded the Distinguished Alumnus Award from the School of Arts & Sciences, University of Washington, Seattle, and five years later was one of fifty alumni to be presented with the "150th Anniversary Timeless Award." A past winner of the Kansas Governor's Arts Award, in 2008, he was designated the first Kansas Master Artist and the same year was honored by the Asian American Arts Alliance, New York City as one of their "Exceptional People in Fashion, Food & the Arts." In 2011 Shimomura was designated a United States Artist. The next year he delivered the commencement address to Garfield High School, Seattle, his alma mater, then was elected to the school's Hall of Fame.

During his teaching career at the University of Kansas he was the first faculty member ever to be designated a University Distinguished Professor (1994), receive the Higuchi Research Prize (1998) and the Chancellor's Club Career Teaching Award (2002). In 2004 he retired from teaching and started the Shimomura Faculty Research Support Fund, an endowment to foster faculty research in the Department of Art.

Shimomura's work is in the permanent collections of over 125 museums nationwide including the Metropolitan Museum of Art, Whitney Museum of American Art, Los Angeles County Museum, Museum of American Art, and the National Portrait Gallery, Smithsonian Institution.

Artist's Statement:

roger shimomura

Artist, Writer, Director & Producer

During the 1960s, while I was a student at the University of Washington, I participated in several wildly popular activities called "happenings." After transferring to the graduate program at Syracuse University, I introduced this concept to my fellow freshman students by asking them to perform an original activity that was thought-provoking and whose potential meaning might emerge well after it was performed. Simultaneous to this form of expression, I took a graduate filmmaking course that left an indelible impression upon me. My fascination with time-lapse content was first reflected in my graduate thesis presentation, which was a multimedia performance that I titled "The Pop Culture and Andy Warhol." The performance drew regional interest by local media and was televised all throughout central New York, but only after newscasters' heavy editing removed my fake interview with Andy Warhol regarding the five-minute "Warhol-style" film I created and claimed to discover in the depths of the New York Public Library as one of Warhol's Factory productions.

After graduating in 1969, I accepted a position on the faculty of the University of Kansas (KU) to teach drawing and painting. After a few years, I asked to teach a basic 3-D design class to further explore my interest in time-based activities, and I was also coveting the new video equipment the department had acquired. In 1985, I purchased my own video camcorder, and shortly thereafter I introduced myself to local choreographer and dancer Marsha Paludan who was teaching in the dance department at KU. Every Wednesday evening, Paludan would bring one or two of the dancers in her troupe to my spacious studio in Lawrence. There, for several hours, we would experiment with my video equipment and play music ranging from funk and classical to modern dance and Kabuki, all while wearing dime-store Halloween costumes and kimonos, to invent short but sassy dance routines. Then, unexpectedly, we received an invitation to perform at the annual Symposium of Contemporary Music at KU, which in turn led to my writing the first act of the *Seven Kabuki Plays*.

Simultaneous to all this, I began teaching performance art in the art department in 1985 and continued until my retirement in 2004. This class became one of the core offerings in the field of expanded media and ultimately became a degree-granting major. During the first expanded media classes, I met Joel Sanderson, a student who was to become the key member of the technical support crew for my performances. His technical expertise and unfailing devotion to these productions were an invaluable part of the total effort. I credit Joel with constantly raising the bar higher and speaking out for wider exposure of our performances. Were it not for his involvement, the production schedule may never have gone past the first presentation.

My gratitude also goes to Marsha Paludan, mentioned earlier, for her patience in nurturing me and supplying the performances with her talented troupe of dancers and performers. Her critical eye and experience assured a professional level of presentation every time. A special nod goes to Tony Allard, a solo performer in the well-traveled *Campfire Diary*, who put up with so many long hours of planning and late rehearsals.

While some of the early performances looked back to some very early issues of Japanese America, much of the work began to focus upon the World War II incarceration of Japanese Americans. Thanks to Kimiko and Akira Yamamoto, both faculty members at KU, their feedback on all things Japanese, including translations of my grandmother's diaries and other writings, brought a critical dimension to the scriptwriting. Over the years, new performers came and went, but Joel, Marsha, and Tony faithfully performed when called upon. I constantly sought grant money, and every performance required host institutional support. Finally, in 2004, I felt it was time to return to painting full time, and now, fourteen years later, in this project I attempt to chronicle those events.

Writer Krystal Reiko Hauseur and I met when she decided to write on my performances in partial fulfillment of the requirements for her M.A. at San Francisco State University. She has since received her Ph.D. in visual studies from the University of California, Irvine. I was so thoroughly impressed with the quality of her writing that I hoped she would be willing and available to write the main text of this book. Given her current status as a wife, the mother of two young children, and the owner of a start-up business, it was generous of her to take on this project.

Thanks also to graphic designer Erin Shigaki for her outstanding design work and to Page Tanagi who established the graphic framework for this book. I am indebted to photographer Veretta Cobler who had the arduous task of digitizing photographs from a chaotic mass of images collected from different sources. A full list of participants follows. Despite its length, I am sure to have left out some people, and to them I sincerely apologize.

List of Participants

In recognition of their contributions toward the creation of my thirteen performances shown in over thirty venues across the nation during an eighteen-year period, I would like to extend my deepest gratitude to the following individuals. Their professional talents range from lighting, sound, choreography, opera, composing, kurogo, performance, documentary film, creative writing, and beyond. This publication honors their collaboration and dedication to my body of performance art. Arigatou! —RS

Allard, Tony
Avanti
Bass, Mary Lynn
Bettinger, Debbie
Bocock, Raina
Brown, Laura
Bui, Kim
Cheng, Debbie
Cheng, Gloria
Cheng, Helen
Cheng, Martin
Christillis, Dennis
Comeau, Jennifer
Covington, Bill
Crabtree, Mark
Craemer, Daniel
Criner, David
Curtis, Mike
Darvik, Roy
Davidson-Hues, Janet
Deshler, Michael
Doni Marie
Ehrlich, Connie
Esrafily, Farrah
Falconer, Elizabeth
Fister, Pat
Fong, Kuang-Yu
Fujita, Jean
Fukada, Kentaro
Gardner, James
Gee, Helen
Gee, Mikka
Gee, Norman
Gilmore, Robin
Gould, Davna
Greene, Lois
Gregoire, Colleen
Gregoire, Tim
Hanna, David
Harris, Sara
Harumoto, Patti
Hauck, Mary
Hollingworth, Sigrid
Hunt, Kelley
Hurst, G. Cameron
Jewell, Jim
Joo, Anna
Kira, Keiko
Kunkel, Charles
Lassley, Dan Patrick
Lewis, Dwayne
Mackender, Gary
Mackender, Greg
McComas, Tony
Monger, Tim
Mott, Teri
Olson, Marty
Osebold, Sara Mariko
Paludan, Kari
Paludan, Marsha

Parrish, Martha
Perry, Kirk
Pike, Mary Lisa
Ramberg, Laura
Reichlin, Joe
Reyes, Poli
Ronning, Karen
Rueff, Sylvie
Sandal, Gwen
Sanderson, Charla
Sanderson, Joel
Schaeffer, James
Shiver, Aaron
Shontz, Jennifer
Smith, Scott
Snyder, Aprylisa
Steuerwald, Alice
Stringer, Jim
Tajima-Peña, Renee
Tamarabuchi, Peter
Templet, Laura
Tsang, Lori
Tsubaki, Andrew
Tullius, Traci
Unruh, Delbert
Unruh, Ione
Vonschlemmeer, Mark
Wachpress, Bill
Wagner, Eric
Wagner, Hans
Wan, Qingli
Weatherford, Jenny
Whitney, Alex
Wildcat, Daniel
Wunch, Michael
Yamamoto, Akira
Yamamoto, Kimiko

preface: roger shimomura's performance art... not made in japan

by Krystal R. Hauseur

For eighteen years, from 1984 to 2002, Roger Shimomura wrote, directed, and produced thirteen performance pieces about the Asian American experience. Shimomura's performances were featured across the nation at thirty-five separate venues, totaling fifty-one shows, and were seen by thousands of people. He received thirteen performance art grants—including two National Endowment for the Arts Fellowships in 1989 and 1991, and a McKnight Interdisciplinary Fellowship in 1995—to support the creation of these works. All thirteen performances are documented and examined individually in this book as a means of introduction to each performance, outlining major themes and stylistic shifts explored by the artist.

Shimomura's artistic methodology and interest in performance can be traced back to his 1969 master of art thesis entitled, "The Pop Culture and Andy Warhol" a combination lecture and performance by Shimomura. While Shimomura's degree was focused on painting, the artist was attuned to and examined the pop art movement, of which Andy Warhol and The Factory were center stage.[1] During the 1960s, traditional art methodology, practice, and institutions were under siege, reflecting the broader social and political unrest in the United States and abroad. Artists, intellectuals, and the broader public challenged conventional thinking, such as seeing the artist's hand, the artist as genius, and notions of authenticity and originality. Shimomura's thesis included a recently discovered Warhol video, titled *Back*, a faux creation by Shimomura of a fellow student's back that the artist supposedly "found" in the New York Public Library. Through performance, Shimomura blurred the line between reality and myth (more specifically stereotype in his postgraduate work), and most importantly, learned a valuable artistic strategy, playing with the signification of meaning, that he would continue to deploy throughout his entire body of work. Shimomura's performance was a carefully orchestrated masquerade that was so outside the boundaries of a conventional M.A. thesis that it almost cost him his degree, were it not for the artist's critical understanding and defense of these avant-garde theories circulating in the Zeitgeist.

Fifteen years passed before Shimomura returned to video and performance art. By the 1980s, both experimental (also called alternative or avant-garde) theater and performance art were flourishing internationally, with several established offshoots. Shimomura's performances sit comfortably in either space of performance art or experimental theater. His pieces can include, but are not limited to, art installations, artwork, scripts, improvisation, audience participation, kurogos,[2] projected slides, video, costume, choreography, acting, historical objects, poems, journals and other primary source documentation, and original music compositions. Performance art (versus experimental theater) is the primary term chosen to describe Shimomura's work because it is not only composed of time, space, performer, and a relationship to the audience, but also because it examines and interrogates a broader array of artistic practices. Furthermore, performance art breaks down the meaning of "traditional western art" and often opposes how it is defined as a productive element of its existence, which is integral to Shimomura's artistic expression.[3] Shimomura uses performance art, similar to pop art, as a way of appealing directly to the public, to shock audiences into reassessing their own notions of art and its relation to culture, especially as it pertains to Asians and Asian Americans, and while Shimomura considers his primary discipline painting, he always finds ways to push the boundary in unexpected directions and evade categorization.

Whether working in the realm of painting, performance art, installation, print, mixed media, or ceramics, Shimomura's signature style is consistently visible because his artistic process and visual strategy remain the same. Shimomura's identity is at the core of his work. As a Sansei—a third-generation Japanese American—Shimomura's work examines representation, difference, and power. Specifically, the artist engages with Orientalism, primarily via stereotypes, and contests this discourse of power by resignifying or calling attention to its mythic and discriminatory forms of racial representation. Shimomura's work examines and disrupts what

Stuart Hall calls the "regime of representation," a less visible form of power that operates in broader cultural and symbolic terms. The regime of representation exercises symbolic power through representational practices such as stereotyping, that represent someone or something a certain way, and fetishism that not only objectifies but also fantasizes what is absent or displaced.

Shimomura's art is disruptive and provocative because it deploys the same systems of meaning-making that mark him as "Other."[4] By accepting and working with the shifting, unstable character of meaning, Shimomura enters, as it were, into a struggle over representation, exposing its constructed nature. Importantly, his strategy always brings the "Gaze"[5] into question, making explicit what is often hidden and operating in the unconscious. Examining the artist's identity through the lens of personal history and the discriminatory ways he is seen by others demonstrates that Shimomura is acutely aware of the power of the Gaze and its ability to construct Otherness—its method of exclusion, its power to split self and other. Shimomura's art goes beyond his personal experience and examines the Japanese American historical narrative because power is circular, meaning it is not only deployed from the top down but also radiates within the dominated and dominant, producing its own discourse of knowledge, and because power is multidimensional and exists in the conscious and unconscious of the subject, affecting past, present, and future histories, memories, and interpretations.

Shimomura plays both sides, so to speak, as he occupies the position of Other to be gazed upon as well as speaking as the Other, as artist and author, bluntly critical of the regimes of representation that have been designed to speak for him. For example, by appropriating *ukiyo-e*[6] (pictures of the floating world) images as exotic—they were unknown to the artist, and they operate symbolically as the embodiment of his Otherness—Shimomura shows the viewer the absurdity of associating such images with his "authentic" identity, articulates the slippage between self and Other, exposes the mythic nature of stereotypes, and shows the disavowal of fetishism. His art, in essence, holds up a mirror and returns the Gaze back upon the regime of representation that attempts to define him as exotic, fetishized, yellow peril, rat bastard, perpetual foreigner, emasculated Asian male, model minority, less than human, Other.

Shimomura's signature style is a visual language the artist creates from juxtaposing historical artifacts from the artist's life, U.S. pop art and culture—including racial images and material culture—and Japanese ukiyo-e and pop culture to represent his experience. Shimomura first explored the way he was seen by mainstream Americans in his *Oriental Masterpiece* paintings by using ukiyo-e prints to signify his Asianness during the early 1970s [IMAGE 1]. Shimomura decided to introduce the exotic ukiyo-e imagery into his work from a conversation the artist had with a local Kansas farmer at an auction, who asked why didn't the artist make art that looked like him. At that moment, Shimomura knew that how he perceived himself (American), and how the farmer perceived him (Asian Other), were vastly different. Shimomura decided at that moment to buy a Japanese coloring book with ukiyo-e prints and began experimenting with their imagery in his work. Up until that point, Shimomura knew next to nothing about Japanese art, had never traveled to Japan (outside of a layover while serving in the U.S. Army), and was a U.S. citizen who grew up loving Disney, Popeye, Dick Tracy, and baseball.

In Seattle, during his first exhibition of the *Oriental Masterpiece* series, his work hung among other works paying tribute to Disney, Buck Rogers, and other pop-culture imagery. Shimomura states, "It was the only painting that 'looked Japanese.' People picked out *Oriental Masterpiece #1* as their favorite and when I asked why, they would say, 'because it looks like you.' This was proof that the painting was effective in the way I had intended and I decided at that point to do more of them. I found that I had control over perpetuating my own 'Otherness' to my audience."[7]

Initially, Shimomura was careful not to make his work narrative, emphasizing design over the political aspects of this imagery, as he was speaking to a fine art audience. However, his exploration unlocked a floodgate of discriminatory representations and racial history that the artist began to collect, consume, deconstruct and reconstruct. These racially charged, material-culture objects unearthed memories from the artist's past, and soon he began juxtaposing them with ukiyo-e, Disney, and comic book characters until he found the same level of emotional tension triggered by an Othering experience from his past. Shimomura built his artistic processes and visual strategy by recreating these experiences, exposing U.S. popular culture's regime of representation, which was devoid of positive images of Asians and Asian Americans.

IMAGE 1: Roger Shimomura, “Oriental Masterpiece #1,” *Oriental Masterpiece Series*, 1971, acrylic on canvas, 60” x 60”, collection of Anonymous.

By the late 1970s, Shimomura quickly abandoned his initial concern of not making art within the boundaries of high art after having the diaries of his grandmother, Toku Shimomura, translated, starting with the years surrounding World War II and the Japanese American incarceration (1942-1945), during which Shimomura, then a toddler and a U.S. citizen, was unconstitutionally imprisoned along with one hundred twenty thousand other Japanese Americans as enemy aliens. Learning Toku’s private feelings, along with his growing collection of discriminatory objects, comic books, and Americana, further inspired Shimomura not only to tell his story, but also to create his own visual lexicon—a signature style that critiqued the regime of representation that sees him as Other.

IMAGE 2: Roger Shimomura, "December 7, 1941," *Diary Series*, 1982, acrylic on canvas, 60" x 50", collection of Anonymous.

IMAGE 3: Roger Shimomura, "Untitled," *Montage Series*, 1985, acrylic on canvas, 60" x 72", collection of the Wichita Art Museum.

Shimomura's first performance, *Toku's Dance* (1984), began as an experimentation with the goal of extending the moment before and after one of the artist's *Diary* series paintings [IMAGE 2].[8] Shimomura drew from his signature image lexicon and incorporated elements of Japanese theater to critique traditional, hierarchical art forms as well as highlight the absurdity of how he is seen as Other. Specifically, in *Toku's Dance*, he chose to open and close the piece using elements from Kabuki , and he invited the dancer Marsha Paludan to collaborate in choreographing the performance. By Shimomura's second performance, the *Seven Kabuki Plays Project* (1985), the artist's paintings were being influenced by his performance work, as directly seen by comparing act seven, "Montage," and the artist's *Montage* series [IMAGE 3]. The visual format, borrowed from film, adds the elements of time and space and serves as a visual way to present different pictorial elements as if they belong together while each element retains its individual identity. Shimomura would continue to deploy several types of visual approaches of seeing—such as comparisons, juxtapositions, semiotics, drag, appropriation, and reification—through experimentation with performance and video to critique the dominant U.S. mainstream media's regime of representation and control over images of Asians and Asian Americans.

Moreover, Shimomura explores other visual and nonvisual art forms, such as music and language. For example, the artist frames each act in the *Seven Kabuki Plays Project* with Toku's diary entry, spoken in Japanese, as the kernel of inspiration for the scene. He not only literally gives Toku a voice, but he also distances the audience from completely understanding Toku's experience and reverses the roles of insider and outsider. With the assistance of Jim Stringer, Joel Sanderson, Elizabeth Falconer, Kari Paludan, and several others, Shimomura composes original soundscapes and music, reimagines iconic American tunes on Japanese instruments, and refashions Orientalist operas and musicals. Costume, set design, lighting, stage, and scene transitions are also reimagined by the artist to suit his trademark style. The artist uses kurogos to facilitate several of the hidden aspects of theater—costume changes, spotlighting, entering, exiting, and performing offstage. Shimomura also plays with the role of the audience through redirecting the Gaze, making them the ones being watched, in *Campfire Diary* (1992), and he later deploys what he terms "subtextual" elements, allowing the audience to participate in the creation of meaning, in *The Last Sansei Story* (1993) and *A Decade of Performances: Not Made in Japan* (1996). With *Amnesia* (2002), Shimomura invites Rene Tajima-Peña to create a video on the loss of memory in *Skate Manzanar,* which he includes in the performance, again subverting the hierarchical role of writer and director. In essence, nothing was off-limits to Shimomura and his deep understanding of the ways in which power operates in the regime of representation.

Performance, as an artistic medium, was critical in Shimomura's execution, reimagining, and shifting of meaning. Furthermore, examining Shimomura's performances alongside his paintings and prints offers deeper insight into the richly textured and layered sources of meaning in his artistic processes as well as the complexities of his identity and experience as an Asian American. For example, he uses Toku's diaries; poems by anonymous Issei[10]; U.S. cultural artifacts; and U.S. and Japanese art, songs, television shows, movie stars, and pop stars. Shimomura takes his visual lexicon and constantly shifts, juxtaposes, and reimagines the players, objects, significations, and relationships—even inserting himself into the work, masquerading as the yellow peril, Superman, George Washington, Dick Tracy, ad infinitum. The artist becomes the superhero or villain and is Japanese, Chinese, American, self, other, real, and fake. He repeatedly moves the boundary, as Shimomura understands that meaning can never be finally fixed, so there can never be any final victories in representation.

Shimomura's artistic pedigree, first as a commercial designer, and then as a pop artist, was cultivated in the crucible of Guy Depord's *Society of the Spectacle*, where reification and commodification transformed lived, bodily experiences through the reproduction of images. Society was becoming increasingly dominated and defined by representations, and importantly, these representations have less to do with the actual world and more to do with the physiological conditions of vision—conditions that can be simulated. Due to the unprecedented mobility of the visual experience, it became abstracted from any founding site or referent. As representations were uprooted, their symbolic power could be manipulated more freely. The mobilization of the Gaze thus promises the mobilization of the self and the transformation of seemingly fixed positions of social identity, but, Shimomura understands, this is always a double-edged sword, part delusion and part promise, all wrapped up in one.

As a contemporary pop artist, Shimomura, like Warhol, utilized a pop way of seeing, a way to "'feel like an insider," as another disruptive strategy of the regime of representation.[11] As Jonathan Flatley explains in his essay titled "Warhol Gives Good Face," "When we acquire a public persona or identify with public bodies, or consume American brands, we participate in 'utopias of self-abstraction' that enable us to feel as if we have transcended our particularity."[12] Shimomura, through his performative masquerade, gains a certain kind of anonymity in identifying with a body that could be anybody's body. Flatley continues, "Moreover, seeing bodies that are like our own in public spaces assures us that we won't be excluded from publicity because of our bodies [and what they look like], that we will not be marked, excluded, refused."[13] Although Shimomura's intent is not so much to feel like an insider, especially not in terms of assimilation or acculturation, and the artist's body is visibly different, as a racialized body, from the represented bodies of the American public, the artist is attempting to use a pop way of seeing to make visible and public his experience as a Japanese American through his elaborate play with the regimes of representation.

Shimomura not only invents and circulates counterdiscourses to formulate oppositional interpretations to negative (and lack of) representations of Asian Americans, but also to access the elements of publicity (consumption, fandom, and spectatorship) through the notion of mourning. Andy Warhol, Ondrej Warhola, was an American-born son of Slovakian-immigrant working class parents; through his artistic strategy of mourning and publicity, he managed to shed his immigrant, outsider, Otherness and become the most iconic American artist. Flatley describes the process of becoming public as acquiring distance from oneself, a "self-negativity...like attending your own funeral. You got to see yourself reified, eulogized, coherent, whole—and you get to see other people recognizing you."[14] Warhol was a master at capitalizing on rebranding famous stars and iconic American brands through the process of visual consumption and in turn making himself and his audience (fans) feel like insiders. Warhol's Marilyn portraits are a remembrance of the famous star; the recognition of her face becomes a placeholder for her life and the publicity she holds in America's collective imagination. Jacques Lacan tells us the work of mourning is a masquerade; the function of the mask is to inscribe and wear a melancholic identification in and on the body. Warhol's Marilyn portraits operate as a mask, and through Warhol's consumption and incorporation of Marilyn, they become Warhol. Part of the affective payback of consumption, like Warhol's Campbell Soups, is the way that, in consuming a product, we can identify ourselves with everyone else who consumes that product; we access another mode of universalizing ourselves and our desires. Through consuming Campbell Soup, mourning Marilyn's death, and appropriating Warhol's art, we become part of a shared public.

IMAGE 4: Roger Shimomura, "Kabuki Party," 1988, serigraph, ed. 40, 12" x 24", collection of the artist.

Shimomura, as a pop artist, taps into notions of publicity and mourning in the public's imagination. Keenly aware of Warhol's artistic strategy, Shimomura appropriates Warhol's Marilyn and Liz paintings into his work as recognition of this pop way of seeing, and he masquerades with the mythmaking status of the artist and consumption of the artist's fame in our culture [IMAGE 4]. By repeatedly producing self-portraits, Shimomura feeds the public's need, its imagination, to see and consume him, and he creates a gap between his reified (public) images and actual (private) self. In this space, with the mask he creates, Shimomura is able to shift meaning and access elements of publicity to disrupt the regime of representation that controls images of Asian Americans. Moreover, a large segment of Shimomura's work is centered on mourning, specifically of his grandmother's life and death and more broadly the Issei, as well as the artist's own preoccupation with his mortality (he is often shown taking his blood pressure), and finally, via performances like *The Last Sansei Story*, which explore his (and the Sansei population's) complete detachment from Japanese culture. Other topics, captured in Shimomura's *Stereotypes and Admonitions* series, draw directly from local media (but are often not well known nationally), such as the racial violence against Asian Americans through the horrific and brutal death

IMAGE 5: Roger Shimomura, “Vincent Chin Murder,” *Stereotype and Admonitions Series*, 2002, acrylic on canvas, 20” x 24”, collection of Anonymous.

of Vincent Chin, in *Vincent Chin Murder*, 2003 [IMAGE 5]. Shimomura’s art builds a public by shining a brighter light on the experiences of Asian Americans and bringing publicity to aspects of a collective U.S. history that is often unknown.

Shimomura’s art exposes several systems of meaning-making to articulate the construction of identity and the instability of any signification. For example, Shimomura exposes the Gaze that fragments him into a collection of parts—slanted eyes, yellow skin, bucktooth, samurai—and fetishizes him from a whole human being into an object of parts. Fetishism involves a disavowal in which a powerful fascination or desire is both indulged and at the same time denied. In terms of representation and Shimomura’s art, *Mix and Match: No. 1* (print, 2001), based on *Match, No Mix: No. 1* (print, 1993) and part of the installation/performance *Yellow Potluck/Fortune Cookies Are*

IMAGE 6: Roger Shimomura, "Mix and Match: No. 1," *Mix and Match Series*, 2001, lithograph, 12" x 9", printer Lawrence Lithography Workshop.

Not Japanese (1994), uses the same visual format (two pairings of kissing couples) and examines the same forever-foreigner stereotype. Comparing the two works, Shimomura remains consistent with his trademark style, shifting the roles of the performers and the signification of meaning.

Mix and Match: No. 1 (2001) uses the slant-eyed, bucktoothed, uncivilized, desexualized stereotype of Asian males, in the super flat, comic book graphic, pop art style (another layer of Shimomura's stylistic objectification) to mix with a prototypical blond-haired comic book heroine [IMAGE 6]. While the kiss is not granted, the couple on the left, featuring an ukiyo-e courtesan and a blond-haired male, are shown mixing and matching. Reading through the lens of fetishism, fantasy intervenes, where what is shown and seen can only be understood in relation to what cannot be seen. Taken as a whole, *Mix and Match: No. 1* both shows and does not show the act of intercultural mixing. The ambivalent desire to be satisfied with what is declared different is at the same time obsessively enjoyed because it is exotic, while being unfulfilled because it is forbidden. Shimomura is also exposing the gender power imbalance of the colonizing white European male, who is permitted to mix with the exotic Other female, and the colonized Asian male, who is never portrayed as a whole human to be accepted by the white female. The double standard in *Mix and Match* is an ambivalence toward difference, both in representing and not representing the tabooed, dangerous, or forbidden object of pleasure and desire. Shimomura's subtle decisions pertaining to looking, such as showing the viewer the stereotyped Asian male and American female faces of the couple on the right, but obscuring the Asian female and American male's faces on the left, remind us that there is often a sexual element in looking, where looking is often driven by an unacknowledged search for illicit pleasure and a desire that cannot be filled.

When interpreted through the lens of stereotypes, Shimomura's use of racist imagery in *Mix and Match: No. 1* directly speaks to discriminatory attitudes that are often unseen and fears that are unspoken, making explicit what is often hidden. This work implies the fear of Asians intermixing with Americans that is evident in antimiscegenation laws, such as the 1922 Cable Act that revoked U.S. citizenship to anyone marrying an Issei all the way up to the 1967 *Loving v. Virginia* case in which the U.S. Supreme Court ruled such laws as unconstitutional. In the portrayal of Asians and Asian Americans as perpetual foreigners, Shimomura exposes the unconscious fears within the stereotypes of Asians as Others, yellow peril, or unhuman. Stereotypes operate where there are gross inequalities of power by affixing difference, creating Otherness, and deploying a strategy of splitting. By reducing, essentializing, naturalizing, and fixing difference, stereotypes divide the normal and the acceptable from the abnormal and the unacceptable and then exclude everything that does not fit—that which is different. Shimomura exposes how stereotypes operate, reveals colonial history, highlights the imbalance of gender, and asks viewers to reflect on the unconscious associations with Asians and Asian Americans created by the regime of representation.

Compared to *Match, No Mix: No. 1* (1993) a much earlier presentation by the artist on the same topic, in which an ukiyo-e couple kiss and an American couple kiss—as the title suggests, matching but not mixing—Shimomura taps into the visualization of Otherness that he experiences as an Asian American and expresses the inability to mix, the unspoken social rules, the lack of multiculturalism, and especially the difficulties he experiences in attempting to reconcile two divergent aspects of his ethnic identity [IMAGE 7]. Shimomura inserts *Match, No Mix: No. 1* into his installation/performance

IMAGE 7: Roger Shimomura, "Match, No Mix: No. 1," *Match, No Mix Series*, 1993, lithograph, 12" x 17", printer Lawrence Lithography Workshop.

Yellow Potluck/Fortune Cookies Are Not Japanese. Here the artist adds more layers of meaning through various theories of looking. *Yellow Potluck* is an installation commissioned by Creative Time, New York, to participate in the Forty-Second Street Art Project that created round-the-clock art installations and galleries to make over Manhattan's Times Square.[15] The gentrification effort transformed a seedy area overrun with pornographic stores into wholesome family entertainment. The project itself was a type of remasking or rebranding of a business district. Constructed as two side-by-side window boxes, Shimomura created public and private spaces in each window to showcase what happens behind closed doors. On the right side, Shimomura shows an Asian American male assimilated to American life but seen as Other, with the *Match, No Mix* print hanging on his wall, while the left side shows an American female who adorns herself with Japanese items, displaying her refinement and worldliness, but she carries a bag full to the brim with racial images of Asians, alluding to discriminatory attitudes she carries. *Yellow Potluck* examines the contradiction of U.S. cultural values, such as democracy, equality, freedom of expression, and the touting of its cultural diversity—yet the need for movements such as multiculturalism and identity politics demonstrates the imbalances and existence of institutional racism, lack of cultural diversity, inequality, and injustice that continue to affect people of color.

Shimomura then adds to this installation, with the help of Kwang Yu Fong, a Peking Chinese Opera actor and performance artist, the performance *Fortune Cookies Are Not Japanese*. Through opera, choreography, costume, and fortune cookies, Shimomura demonstrates how symbols (like fortune cookies) that we think are foreign are inventions of a mythmaking apparatus; fortune cookies were invented in California and are a construction of ethnicity/Asianness/Other. Dan Wildcat's song, from *The Last Sansei Story*, says it best: "Yellow all same, yellow no same. / It does not matter. What's in a name? / Yellow all the same; yin is the game." Tracing the singular thread of being seen and represented as forever foreign through Shimomura's oeuvre *Match, No Mix* reveals the symbolic power of the regime of representation that the artist challenges, repeatedly, through multiple and complex lenses. Shimomura uses a stereotypical image of Asians to talk about the way they are seen, their Otherness, antimiscegenation laws, hidden fears, American ideals, constitutional rights, social norms, multiculturalism, and identity politics that affect Asians and Asian Americans, both past and present.

Shimomura's performance work was not the first to deal with the Japanese American or, more broadly, the Asian American experience. The cultural movements of the late sixties and early seventies, spawned by the Civil Rights movement, catalyzed profound change among U.S. citizens and immigrants, inspiring them to dig into their pasts and tell their stories, and these stories continue to expand and enrich our collective U.S. history. In the 1960s, four theater groups focusing on the narrative and physical presence of Asian America emerged: the East West Players of Los Angeles, the Asian American Theater Workshop (later named the Asian American Theater Company) of San Francisco, the Pan Asian Repertory Theater of New York City, and the Theatrical Ensemble of Asians (renamed Northwest Asian American Theater) of Seattle. Each of these four Asian American theater groups fought to improve the presence of Asian Americans in its respective community locale as well as on a national scale by fighting racism in the entertainment industry, writing plays about the Asian American experience, and producing them in off-Broadway shows. Their invaluable collective work was aimed at disrupting the mainstream theater and entertainment cultures that had systematically excluded Asian American performers and their stories.

Shimomura's work was neither directly attempting to create more acting roles for Asian Americans (although his work does address the visual discrimination and lack of presence of Asian Americans in mainstream media) nor to win awards for best playwright, like David Henry Hwang's *M. Butterfly*, which received a Tony Award for best play. The Asian American Theater groups and playwrights were already tackling this invaluable work across the nation. Shimomura's audience was aligned more closely with the art world (as opposed to theater, Broadway, and entertainment), as his visual language is rooted in pop art and his artistic process in dadaism through the collecting of material culture and rejection of mainstream capitalist society and aestheticism. Moreover, Shimomura's performances are more closely associated to the realm of performance art and experimental theater.

Solo performance was another form of intervention into the structure and expression of Asian American performance art that emerged in the 1970s, which included artists such as Dan Kwong, Denise Uyehara, Jude Narita, and Lane Nishikawa, to name a few. While Shimomura's work does not fall into this type of performance art, he has inserted himself into some of his performances, most notably the lecture/performance for his master's thesis and, later, in *A Decade of Performances, Not Made in Japan* (on the occasion of his distinguished professor designation). The importance of inserting the artist's body into the performance is not a central focus as a means of subversion (such as body art) and does not operate in the same manner as his paintings, where masquerade and Shimomura's shifting occupation of various identities is a destabilizing strategy of his visual semiotics.

Shimomura's performances have been featured in major venues such as the Smithsonian Institution, National Museum of American History, Walker Art Center, and Franklin Furnace. No other Asian American artist, with the exception of Ping Chong, was creating performance art (or in Chong's case, experimental theater works) on a national scale. In 1975, Chong founded Ping Chong & Company in order to explore the meaning of contemporary theater and art on a national and international scale by creating and touring innovative multidisciplinary work. Chong is a pioneering Chinese American multimedia artist who chose to pursue alternative or experimental theater in the early 1970s. While aesthetically Shimomura's and Chong's performances are different, they share similar concerns through the interaction of Asian and Western cultures and draw on documentary and interview-based materials. Also, Chong incorporates theatrical elements such as visual effects, sound control, dance, mime, and spectacle, based on his interest in

Cantonese opera. Shimomura similarly incorporates Kabuki techniques as modes of intervention into traditional western theatrical forms in order to express his "Asianness" to mainstream America. However, Shimomura's artistic expressions predominantly examine the artist's personal identity and Asian American history from his point of view and through his signature style. Despite different formal approaches, both Shimomura and Chong participate in experimental theater by departing from traditional hierarchical methods of creating theater—writer, director, actor, audience—and see performers as creative agents in themselves, along with deploying different uses of language, sound, and the body to not only change the mode of perception but also to create a new relationship to the audience.

Beyond removing the mask of representation, Shimomura's message throughout all of his art is to foster a greater sensitivity to differences—especially cultural differences. His performances are critical to understanding the role-playing and shifting of meaning at the core of his work. Shimomura uses mourning, drag, pun, humor, branding, publicity, appropriation, symbolism, semiotics, juxtaposition, and performance to expose the discrimination and stereotypes encountered by Asian Americans. Regardless of medium (painting, performance, or print), Shimomura's art is fundamentally pop. The artist's stylistic approach and visual strategy are rooted in pop culture and have always been geared toward the mainstream U.S. audience and American art world. Shimomura not only attacks the symbolic power of stereotypes, but he also plays with the notion of "looking" by calling attention to its processes of signification, to make it strange and defamiliarize it. He draws on the desires and ambivalence of fetishism; deploys humor to laugh with, not at, his characterizations, exposing their absurdity; and creates counterdiscourses via his symbolic lexicon. Shimomura's pop art engages with publicity by "giving (his) face" to the public through the notions of consumption and mourning. Through his infinite signification of meaning, something new is learned each time it is seen. Beneath his super flat, comic book style, we feel the ethos, pathos, and logos of the artist's Asian American experience. Shimomura's art contributes to a broader representation of American art and history, and it gives a loud and shocking voice to Asian American identity in the U.S. collective imagination. His work fights regimes of representation that belittle and disempower Others and demonstrates that the world is strengthened, not divided, through difference.

Marsha Paludan as Akiko Wada (Photograph by Roger Shimomura, *Trans-Siberian Excerpts*, February 14-15, 1987, Lawrence Art Center: Lawrence, Kansas).

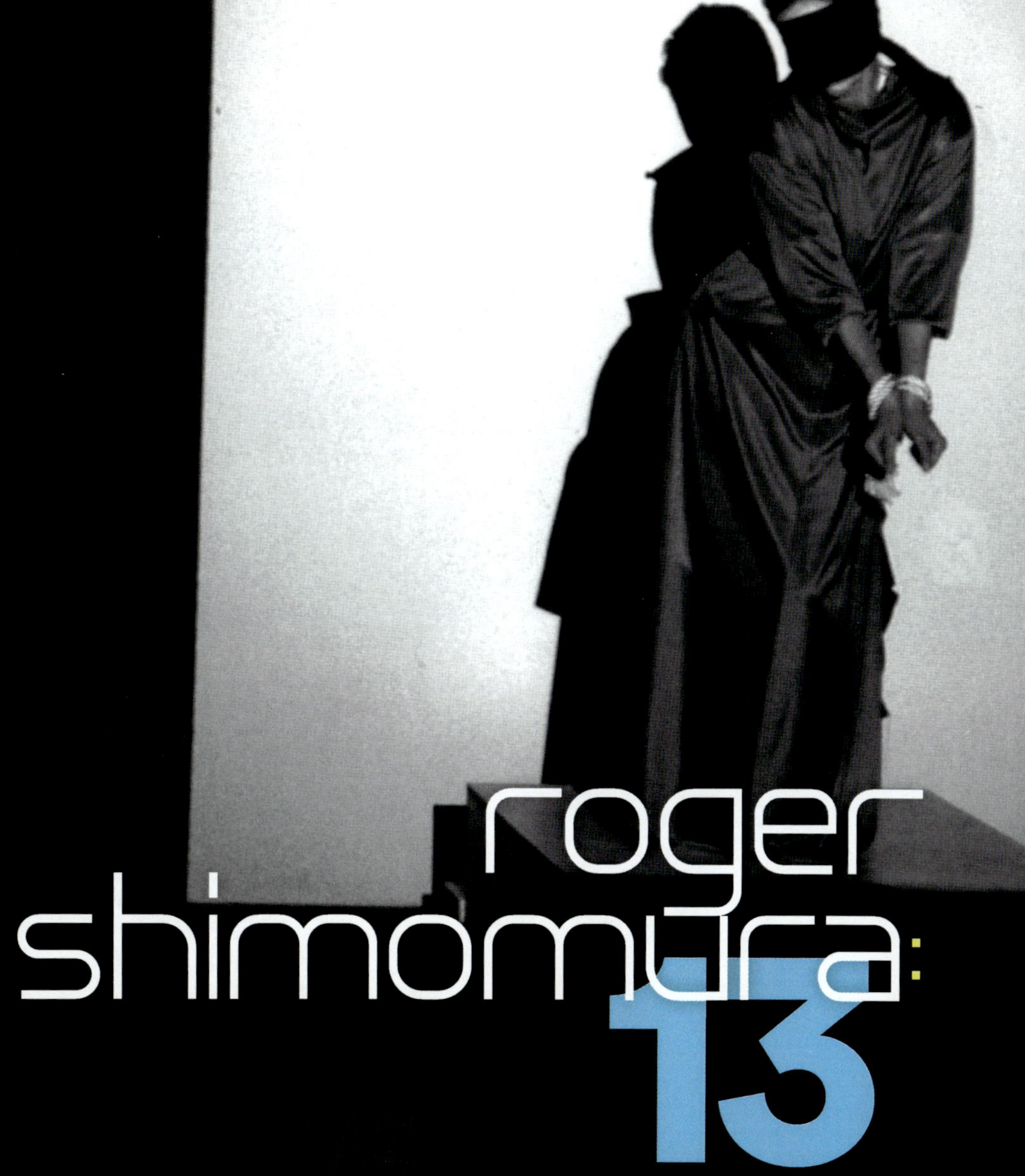

roger shimomura: 13 Performance Pieces

Marsha Paludan as Toku (Photograph by Roger Shimomura, *Toku's Dance*, November 10, 1984, Kellas Gallery: Lawrence, Kansas).

1

toku's dance

• **Kellas Gallery, Lawrence, Kansas, November 10, 1984**

Roger Shimomura's first performance[16] piece, *Toku's Dance*, was a short and simple start to a robust eighteen-year career of richly elaborate and nationally performed performance art pieces. Toku Shimomura was Roger Shimomura's grandmother. *Toku's Dance* was inspired by her recently translated diaries–which documented every day of her life in the United States, beginning in 1912 with her immigration to Seattle, Washington, and ending with her death in 1968[17]–and Shimomura's *Diary Series* paintings. The piece comprises four main elements: Toku, danced by choreographer Marsha Paludan; a kurogo, performed by Colleen Gregoire; a shoji (sliding wall screen that acts as a room divider) set design; and a hybrid audio composition that combined Tyrone Brunson's 1984 release "Servo-Go-Go"[18] and Kabuki music. Start to finish, the piece runs seven minutes.

Toku's Dance begins with the kurogo signaling the attention of the audience by bowing before kneeling stage left. This entrance departs from Kabuki and heightens the audience's awareness of Shimomura's use of Japanese-style theater. Toku stands frozen behind a large shoji. She is backlit and dressed in a kimono and Kabuki mask [IMAGE 9]. The kurogo starts to slowly and steadily beat wooden clackers, picking up speed and intensity before suddenly stopping. Then hybrid music begins, and Toku starts dancing behind the screen for approximately two minutes before moving in front of the screen and continuing her dance for another three minutes [IMAGE 10]. The piece ends with Toku returning behind the shoji and the entire stage fading to black, while the kurogo's clacking resumes at a slow, rhythmic pace that accelerates rapidly before ending abruptly.

The clacking sounds are meant to signal the start and end of a performance in Kabuki. Kurogos are a strategic aspect of all of Shimomura's performances because they recognize his Japanese heritage, symbolizing his Japanese American experience and underlining his message to the audience of fostering a greater appreciation of cultural differences. In *Toku's Dance*, the clacking sounds carry additional symbolism representative of Toku's beating

IMAGE 9: Marsha Paludan as Toku (Photograph by Roger Shimomura, *Toku's Dance*, November 10, 1984, Kellas Gallery: Lawrence, Kansas).

heart, as she was a highly influential person in the artist's life, while the hybrid audio reinforces a sensitivity to cultural differences.

The visual imagery, reflective in the set design and Toku's costume, and the use of Kabuki elements such as a mask and a kurogo, are similar to the visual strategy of Shimomura's paintings in which the artist blends iconography from Japanese ukiyo-e wood-block prints and American popular culture—largely comics, Disney characters, and magazines—to interrogate attitudes about race and perceptions of Japanese Americans. The image of a backlit Toku is taken directly from the artist's paintings. Shimomura explains that the impetus for *Toku's Dance* was an exploration of "the implied events implicit both before and after the frozen moment or composition of the painting [specifically, *Diary: December 7, 1941 (Pearl Harbor Day)*, 1980]."[19] Shimomura's painting oeuvre is loaded with the visual history of hypersexualized images of Asian women in U.S. film and popular culture. The backlit Toku provocatively questions notions of Western exoticism of Asian cultures, yet at the same time, Shimomura examines what it feels

IMAGE 10: Marsha Paludan as Toku (Photograph by Roger Shimomura, *Toku's Dance*, November 10, 1984, Kellas Gallery: Lawrence, Kansas).

like to move, perform, and be seen as Toku, a Japanese American female, Shimomura's grandmother, and the primary resource for a large portion of the artist's artwork.

For *Toku's Dance*, the artist experimented and collaborated with choreographer Marsha Paludan for three months. While Shimomura wrote, directed, and designed *Toku's Dance*, the collaborative nature and interpretive freedom given to Paludan are characteristic of performance art and experimental theater, dismantling the traditional, hierarchical format of Western theater for a more collaborative and hybrid method of creation. *Toku's Dance* employs dance, music, and theater to examine notions of cultural authenticity, orientalism, hybridity, and the historical experiences of Japanese Americans.

Marsha Paludan as Toku (Photograph by Roger Shimomura, *Seven Kabuki Plays Project*, March 27, 1987, Richardson Auditorium, Southwestern College: Winfield, Kansas).

seven kabuki plays project 2

- **Act I excerpt, Crafton-Preyer Theater, University of Kansas, Lawrence, Kansas, February 26, 1985**
- **Acts I–III excerpt, White Concert Hall, Washburn University, Topeka, Kansas, June 6, 1985**
- **Acts I–V excerpt, Karl Bruder Theater, Emporia State University, Emporia, Kansas, January 16, 1986**
- **Richardson Auditorium, Southwestern College, Winfield, Kansas, March 27, 1987**

The *Seven Kabuki Plays Project* is Shimomura's first performance art project performed in its entirety on March 27, 1987, at the Richardson Auditorium, Southwestern College, Winfield, Kansas. The seven acts grew sequentially over a two-year period and are directly correlated to Toku Shimomura's translated diaries, beginning with the first act, "December 7, 1941, Pearl Harbor Day," and ending with act VI, "December 25, 1942, Christmas at Minidoka incarceration center, Hunt, Idaho." Act VII, "Montage," is a summation of the six acts. The *Seven Kabuki Plays Project* not only conveys the heightened attitudes and racism experienced by Japanese Americans during World War II that led to their unjust incarceration[20] from 1942 to 1945, but it also offers a visceral first-person account of Toku's life through the structure and performance of theater.

The *Seven Kabuki Plays Project* highlights a truly one-of-a-kind primary source that comprises in its totality fifty-six years and 20,440 entries. Each of the seven acts, with the exception of act VII: "Montage," are framed by a specific diary entry that is read in Japanese (the way Toku's diaries were written) before the act begins. During the course of the act, short segments of Toku's daily entry are translated into English and incorporated into the audio component of the act. Each act is performed by dancers, choreographed by Marsha Paludan, and assisted by kurogos, to an original musical score by Jim Stringer.

Act I, "December 7, 1941," begins similarly to *Toku's Dance* with darkness, the beat of wooden clappers, and Toku dancing in front of a brick wall [IMAGE 12]. However, in the *Seven Kabuki Plays Project*, Shimomura adds

IMAGE 12: Marsha Paludan as Toku (Photograph by Roger Shimomura, *Seven Kabuki Plays Project*, March 27, 1987, Richardson Auditorium, Southwestern College: Winfield, Kansas).

a significant amount of context—such as set design that moves, costumes, lighting, and music—to evoke December 7, 1941, the day Pearl Harbor was attacked by Japan, through the words of a Japanese American woman, Shimomura's grandmother. Toku's first-hand account reads as follows:

> *December 7, 1941: When I came back from church, I heard the dreamlike news that Japanese airplanes had bombed Hawai'i. I was surprised beyond belief. I sat in front of the radio and I listened to the news all day. It was said that this morning at 6 a.m. Japan declared war on the United States. Our future has become gloomy. I pray that God will stay with us.*[21]

For Americans, especially Japanese Americans, this day radically changed the course of their lives forever, as never before had the United States been attacked within its national borders. Toku's diary clearly expresses her shock at the attack on Hawai'i and her refuge in Christianity for protection, which was contrary to the attitudes and actions taken by the U.S. government that questioned Japanese Americans' loyalty to the United States. The stage opens with Toku dancing in front of a brick wall to symbolize Western culture—specifically, the city of Seattle, Washington. As Toku moves across the stage, the set walls change to shoji to reveal the private interior of her Seattle home, symbolizing Shimomura's cultural roots in Japan. Because Toku wears a Kabuki mask, her body and hand movements are expressive of the emotional and psychological angst that Toku, and all Japanese Americans, experienced during this unprecedented life-changing event. As the scene progresses, Shimomura uses music and material culture to recreate Toku's life on that horrific and tragic day. Some of the historically significant symbolic props that Shimomura used were a 1940s art deco radio (now in the collection of the Museum of Modern Art, New York), President Roosevelt's

“Day of Infamy” speech, a Japanese Zero Fighter plane, a twenty-two-foot-tall Superman, and a Methodist cross [IMAGES 13-16]. Shimomura describes himself as a “collector of many eclectic things,” and his use of historically accurate objects in his work, coupled with his desire to collect these objects, is highly important to the artist’s creative process.[22] The tension and boundary between the real and imagined are critical themes throughout all of the artist’s work—and an ideal space in which to elicit a viewer’s change of perception.

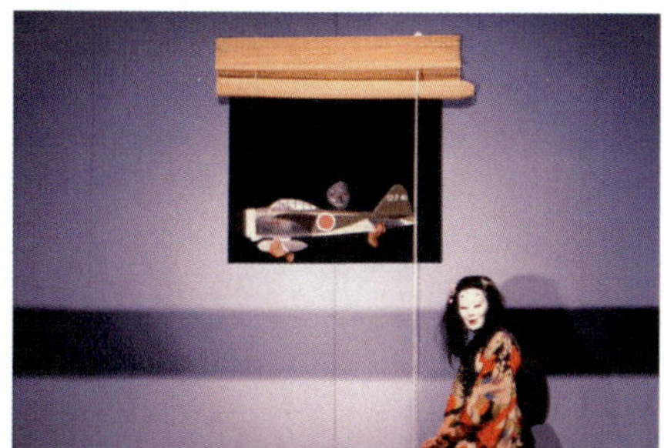

Top left and right, IMAGES 13 and 14: Marsha Paludan as Toku.

Bottom, IMAGE 15: Marsha Paludan as Toku with 27 foot tall Superman.

(All photographs by Roger Shimomura, *Seven Kabuki Plays Project*, March 27, 1987, Richardson Auditorium, Southwestern College: Winfield, Kansas).

Act II, "December 12, 1941," and act III, "February 3, 1942," focus on important historical events pertaining to the treatment of Japanese Americans by the U.S. government. After hearing Toku's diary entry in Japanese, act II opens with Toku having her blood pressure taken, then stating, "My blood pressure was 190...Starting from today we were permitted to withdraw $100 from the bank [IMAGE 17]." One of the civil liberties that was taken from all Japanese Americans was access to their income as their bank accounts were frozen after Pearl Harbor, December 7, 1941. Another infringement of civil liberty was the mandated documentation of all Japanese Americans based on their ethnicity that resulted in their unjust imprisonment, loss of personal income, and forfeiting of rights as U.S. citizens.[23] It is highly plausible that Toku's dark humor was shared by Shimomura's stylistic approach and ironic visual codings, such as Superman's second appearance as representative of the U.S. government's "large-heartedness," that Toku describes when she is granted access to personally earned money [IMAGE 18].

In act III, "February 3, 1942," Toku describes building up her courage to go to the post office with Mrs. Sasaki and complete her fingerprint registration: "We finished the *strict* registration at 11:00 a.m. (author's emphasis)." Toku's diary entry continues to describe that she "finally decided" to comply with the government's mandate and that "a heavy load" was taken off her mind, implying that she had an opportunity to rebel. During the act, Shimomura projects Toku's fingerprint, marking not only the performer's body but also the entire stage before spinning the copies of the fingerprint projection in circles to effect a crazed, psychedelic state of mind. Symbolically, Shimomura highlights the magnitude of uncertainty and wartime hysteria that Toku faced and the surreality of this moment in her life [IMAGE 19]. Literally, the identity of all Japanese Americans was turned upside down from citizen to enemy of the state, landowner to homeless, employed to

IMAGE 16: Marsha Paludan as Toku (Photograph by Roger Shimomura, *Seven Kabuki Plays Project*, March 27, 1987, Richardson Auditorium, Southwestern College: Winfield, Kansas).

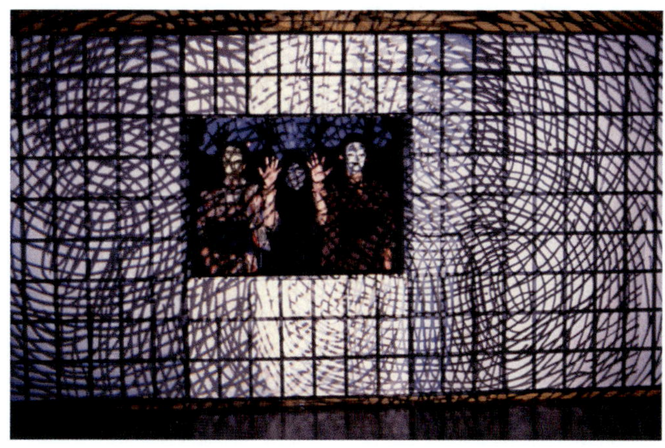

Top, IMAGE 17: Marsha Paludan as Toku.

Center, IMAGE 18: Marsha Paludan as Toku.

Bottom, IMAGE 19: Marsha Paludan as Toku and Laura Ramberg as Mrs. Sasaki.

(All photographs by Roger Shimomura, *Seven Kabuki Plays Project*, March 27, 1987, Richardson Auditorium, Southwestern College: Winfield, Kansas).

IMAGE 20: Marsha Paludan as Toku and Robin Gilmore as Evil Queen.

IMAGE 21: Kurogos Carrying Bologna and Hotdogs.

unemployed, free to prisoner, individual to nameless collective, with family to forcefully separated, and the list continues. The war, in combination with the actions of the U.S. government, contributed to Toku's high blood pressure, which she documents in her diary entries on a frequent basis; it also alludes to her profession as a nurse in Japan and a midwife in Seattle before being incarcerated.

"The Interlude" between acts III and IV recreates the forced relocation to the ten imprisonment centers that all Japanese Americans living on the West Coast experienced. Act IV, "August 27, 1942"; act V, "May 21, 1942"; and act VI, "December 25, 1942," address the incarceration experience through climate conditions and dietary health. In act IV, Toku describes the harsh environments characteristic of all ten incarceration centers, which were located in desolate and uninhabitable landscapes. The audience feels Toku's anger when she describes the weather: "Storm. What a view! I have never seen such a dust storm. It was so dark we were all afraid to move. Pessimistic words came out of everyone's mouth. We were sent to such a harsh place!" The tar-paper barracks, straw mattresses, cloth room dividers, single coal-burning furnace per barracks building (not family), and one suitcase allotment per internee, left little opportunity for appropriate insulation, heating, or attire. Similar to the loaded iconography found in his painting, Shimomura draws from Disney by using a nine-foot-tall open-mouthed head of Cinderella to pull barbed wire across the stage to begin act IV, and he humorously incorporates a dancing evil queen to close the act [IMAGE 20]. Although Disney did not produce its own version of Cinderella, a seventeenth-century story, until 1950, it is hard not to consider Shimomura's personal experience of incarceration as a young child, three

IMAGE 22: Laura Ramberg as Santa Claus.

IMAGE 23: Marsha Paludan as Toku.

(All photographs by Roger Shimomura, *Seven Kabuki Plays Project*, March 27, 1987, Richardson Auditorium, Southwestern College: Winfield, Kansas).

years old, and the inclusion of his memories and the visual language accessible to him during this dark period. When the *Seven Kabuki Plays Project* is examined through this lens, a unique dialogue spanning three generations emerges between Toku's words and Shimomura's imagery.

Act V reveals the limited dietary options, with melancholia and boredom caused over the repeated serving of hotdogs and bologna [IMAGE 21]. Toku writes, "Lunch today was wieners, and once again for dinner it was bologna. I had a poor appetite." While superficially this journal entry appears mundane and—coupled with Shimomura's presentation of dancing, human-sized wieners and bologna through the aisle and up onto the stage—is darkly comical, Shimomura and Toku address a systematic aspect of incarceration that affected all aspects of life: extreme lack of resources, such as food, medicine, living facilities, news, creative outlets, socialization, urban environments, culture, private space, personal belongings, and the unhealthiness that all this caused. Being imprisoned without just cause was physically and mentally debilitating to over one hundred twenty thousand people, even resulting in the deaths of children—such as Shimomura's sibling, Carolyn, who died of meningitis while incarcerated.

Act VI is more celebratory as it examines the strength and conviction of Japanese Americans to continue living their lives according to their own determination [IMAGES 22-23]. Despite being uprooted from her home, community, and livelihood and then grouped together with over ten thousand people she had never met before in an incarceration center, Toku was able to create and participate in the joy and blessings of Christmas Day. She writes:

IMAGE 24: Marsha Paludan as Toku and Kurogo (Photograph by Roger Shimomura, *Seven Kabuki Plays Project*, March 27, 1987, Richardson Auditorium, Southwestern College: Winfield, Kansas).

> *The muddy ground was completely covered by the snow. It was like a beautiful white cloth and was a suitable sight for Christmas. The dinner was in mess hall number 7. The waitresses and cooks were all dressed up in the beautifully decorated mess hall. The radio emitted melodies of Christmas. We happily sat at our family table. At 9:00 p.m. Santa Claus appeared. For these few moments, I forgot where I was.*[24]

This moment was made possible by the collective planning of all internees, working together and pooling their resources to make this holiday feel as though they were still living in their homes and experiencing the lives from which they'd been taken. Toku's entry demonstrates the humanity and perseverance of the internees, who lived their lives on their own terms through these small acts, despite the challenging and desperate circumstances they now faced.

Act VII, "Montage," is based on a painting technique that Shimomura uses in his *Untitled* series, which has its roots in surrealism. By combining the content of acts I through VI, Shimomura's act VII is symbolic of Toku's memory flashing before the audience [IMAGES 24-25]. This was the first time Shimomura used this narrative technique and structure in theater to tell his grandmother's story. The artist likely devised this fragmented format in

IMAGE 25: Laura Ramberg as Santa Claus (Photograph by Roger Shimomura, *Seven Kabuki Plays Project*, March 27, 1987, Richardson Auditorium, Southwestern College: Winfield, Kansas).

part from the experimental video art he created as a graduate student at Syracuse University.

Shimomura was part of a select few playwrights in the 1980s who addressed the incarceration of over one hundred twenty thousand Japanese Americans, of which approximately two-thirds were U.S. citizens by birth who had their constitutional rights taken away.[25] Shimomura was unique in his theater style as he blended Japanese and Western theater structures paralleling the formalist strategy that he deployed in his paintings—a hybrid visual language that combined Japanese and U.S. popular-culture imagery to foster dialogue about the Japanese American experience. Shimomura incorporates several components of Kabuki into the *Seven Kabuki Plays Project*, including Kabuki's foundational origins in dance, the use of *hanamachi* (a passageway that extends from the back of the audience to the stage), and a revolving stage and tear-apart set design that allowed scene changes occurring before the audience without needing to close a curtain.[26] Even the development from one singular performance into a group of several short acts mimics the evolution of Kabuki during the three centuries spanning the Edo period. Characteristically, Shimomura's use of melodrama, humor, and popular culture is also visible at this time in both his performance pieces and paintings.

Marsha Paludan as Junko (singer)
(Photograph by Roger Shimomura, *Trans-Siberian Excerpts*, February 14-15, 1987, Lawrence Art Center: Lawrence, Kansas).

trans-siberian excerpts 3

- **Lawrence Arts Center, Lawrence, Kansas, February 14–15, 1987**
- **Grand Ballroom, Eastern Illinois University, Charleston, Illinois April 24–25, 1987**
- **Cleveland Public Theater, Cleveland, Ohio, April 2, 1988**
- **Louis J. Roussel Performance Hall, Loyola University, New Orleans, Louisiana, March 17, 1989**

Trans-Siberian Excerpts was inspired by Shimomura's eight days of travels across seven time zones riding on the Trans-Siberian Railway, in May of 1986. The Trans-Siberian Railway is the world's longest railway (5,753 miles), spanning the continents of Europe and Asia. Shimomura began his journey in Beijing and ended it in Moscow, taking in landscapes such as the Great Wall of China, Outer and Inner Mongolia, the Gobi Desert, and Lake Baykal. Shimomura was inspired to ride the Trans-Siberian Railway after reading *The Big Red Train Ride*, by Eric Newby (1979), a travelogue of Newby's heavily policed and censored journey across the Soviet Union, during Communist rule, as a British foreigner.[27] Shimomura wanted to create a performance piece that reflected a continuous, uninterrupted span of time. During his travels, Shimomura composed twenty performances. But after completion abroad and one week into his return to the United States, the artist's tote bag—full of his scripts, notes, one hundred Polaroid photos, three hundred unopened picture slides, and audiocassettes—was stolen from his locked van in Seattle.[28] He recreated eighteen of the twenty performance pieces, but two were lost forever, and to this day, his only evidence of this journey is a single Polaroid he sent to his mother during his travels.

Trans-Siberian Excerpts is composed of eight short film and performance pieces varying from four to fifteen minutes in length. Shimomura was concerned with issues of cultural morality, oppressive government policy, and identity. The artist drew parallels between Newby's account of Communist Russia and his Japanese American experience, as the Trans-Siberian Railway is a physical link between Europe and Asia and a symbolic link between the constructed binary of the East and the West. While the eight performances that comprise *Trans-Siberian Excerpts* are divergent in subject matter, media, and composition, all of the pieces were influenced by melodramatic theater, which the artist punctuates with his distinctive use of dark humor and parody.

The opening sequence situates the audience in the U.S.S.R. during the 1970s, referencing Newby's travelogue and Shimomura's later travel along the Trans-Siberian Railway, the primary impetuses for this body of performance art [IMAGE 27]. Fog fills the theater, lights are off, two searchlights scan the room, and the sound of a running train permeates the room as the audience is invited to take their seats. Two kurogos dressed as Soviet soldiers march across the aisles and up to the stage, maneuvering their rifles against the backdrop of two Soviet flags. During their performance, the audio shifts from a militaristic beat to Russian folk music. On stage, the kurogos change costumes and now are dressed in kimonos and Kabuki masks. The backdrop changes to two flags of Japan, and the audio shifts to funky Japanese folk music as the kurogos dance across the stage visual and back down the aisle to the back of the auditorium before changing into their all-black costumes.

IMAGE 27: Detail (Photograph by Roger Shimomura, *Trans-Siberian Excerpts*, February 14-15, 1987, Lawrence Art Center: Lawrence, Kansas).

While the train is symbolic of Western modernization, and the railway symbolizes the cultural exchange between two vast continents—Europe and Asia—Shimomura examines the clandestine meanings that emerge from the cultural intersections catalyzed by the world's longest railway. Specifically, the artist draws parallels to the Japanese Americans' experience and their immigration linking two divergent cultures, the United States and Japan, with the effects of World War II through the Japanese American incarceration—which demolished their economic, social, and political rights—and the atomic bombs dropped on Hiroshima and Nagasaki that annihilated the two cities and their inhabitants and severed the connections maintained by the Issei and Kibei Nisei[29] (one and a half generation) immigrants to their relatives in Japan.

Set Me Free

"Set Me Free" is modeled on a song by 1970s Japanese pop singer, Akiko Wada, called "Set Me Free." The entire song is sung in Japanese, with the exception of the words "set me free," which are repeated five times throughout the song in English. Shimomura's appropriation of Wada's song reverses the meaning, as U.S. listeners cannot understand the Japanese subject that Wada hopes to liberate. Shimomura provides his own context through a blindfolded and bound, presumably Japanese American, female performer, and a Chinese American film, titled *Jade Snow*, about a second-generation Chinese American girl raised by a traditional Chinese father in American society. Coupling the lyrics of a Japanese pop singer, performance of a Japanese American female, and a film about a Chinese American female, Shimomura creates a cross-cultural and multigenerational dialogue about the adversities of Asian and Asian American females who navigate history and tradition alongside multiple cultural influences and societal modernization. But Shimomura never reveals the woman's face, allowing the issues raised in the performance to be applicable to any repressed woman.

Similar to the opening sequence, the theater is dark, and twenty-five beats of "Set Me Free" are played before the right side of the stage is illuminated. A woman, blindfolded and with bound hands, wiggles and dances to the beat of the music on a platform. She is dressed in five layers of costume that will be removed after each of the five "set me free" phrases in English is sung—beginning with a long blue nightgown, then a long kimono, a long evening gown, a short kimono, and finally, a miniskirt—with the kurogo's assistance. Alternating between the music and costume changes are clips from the film Jade Snow, featured on the left side of the stage. After a minute, the film stops, the left side of the stage is darkened, and the right side of the stage is reilluminated. The music resumes with the bound and blindfolded dancer continuing her performance. The vacillation between Japanese and Chinese American women progresses until the song has been sung in its entirety. "Set Me Free" takes a clear gender and ethnic focus but artfully opens itself to interpretation and fosters critical discussion of a marginalized subject—the Asian American woman, and her cultural access to her histories and experiences.

What Killed Grandma

"What Killed Grandma" is a video-and-performance piece with a parallel structure to "Set Me Free." On the left side of the stage is a video projection of a 1940s Japanese photo album accompanied by a female voice singing a synthesized and repetitious melody, "Inka Dinka Doo." The melody is a ubiquitous reference to U.S. popular music during the 1940s, such as Jimmy Durante's *Greatest Hits* recording. Pages of the album are slowly turned, revealing photographs of objects, memories, and events that encapsulate Toku's life and may have contributed to her death. The photographs include images of salted salmon; Roger as a child; Toku's son, Mich, who died of a heart attack at age forty-four; Minidoka; Toku's midwife's delivery bag; a crucifix; Meiji wood-block prints; and photographs of the Russo-Japanese War. Each photograph is viewed with the camera panning in and out on each page of the album before the next page is turned, to the accompaniment of the "Inka Dinka Doo" melody. After the viewer has seen six pages, the video cuts to black, and the right side of the stage is illuminated with a Kabuki-masked performer, playing Toku, who takes her blood pressure and sighs in despair. This sequence is repeated three times until the album has been viewed in its entirety, and the piece ends with Toku taking her blood pressure one last time. The audience hears twenty beats of her heart, and then she dramatically collapses on the stage [IMAGE 28].

"What Killed Grandma" is a very dark and direct statement about the unspoken pain and effects of the Japanese American incarceration and Shimomura's personal history. The tone and pace of "What Killed Grandma" is slow and calculated. The artist uses the silence and stillness, along with the hissing of the blood pressure cuff and the heartbeats to evoke uncomfortable and painful feelings in the viewer. In the same vein as the book titled *No-No Boy*, which recounts the unraveling of families and the loss of

IMAGE 28: Marsha Paludan as Toku (Photograph by Roger Shimomura, *Trans-Siberian Excerpts*, February 14-15, 1987, Lawrence Art Center: Lawrence, Kansas).

personal earnings and social networks caused by the incarceration and its aftermath, Shimomura's loss of his grandmother due to hypertension is a grave reminder of the too-often-unspoken and destructive effects that take place long after war has ended. In addition, the artist obsesses over his high blood pressure because it has ailed him throughout his life as well. Similar to "Set Me Free," "What Killed Grandma" is a multigenerational and historical examination, although it's also a deeply personal look into Shimomura's past.

Moon Seen as Exiles

"Moon Seen as Exiles" draws on the absurdity of two events that marked the artist's life. Shimomura uses extreme parody to address an intense tragedy encapsulated in a poem written by a female internee at the Minidoka incarceration center in Hunt, Idaho, where the Shimomura family was incarcerated. The poem captures the climate, isolation, and mental and physical struggles Japanese Americans experienced while being incarcerated. This was the first time this poem was presented before an audience. Shimomura creates a parody of this poem through an absurdity he witnesses at his university: the plight of the University of Kansas Jayhawks' football fans in supporting a team that has never made it to a title game in its entire existence. This style of parody is part of Shimomura's artistic strategy, which uses dark humor to shock and entertain viewers while educating them about historical atrocities. Shimomura uses parody as a tool of mass appeal to have his message widely heard.

"Moon Seen as Exiles" opens with Japanese percussion and shakuhachi music, while Kurogo 1 lights a parasol, held by Kurogo 2, over a masked woman dressed in a kimono who walks slowly with her head bent in defeat and exhaustion. As they move across the stage, the kurogos throw metallic confetti two times before reaching a table prepared for a Japanese tea ceremony. Upon reaching the table, the woman is illuminated by a picture slide of a teapot. In Japanese, the poem is read, and Shimomura's artistically reinterpreted tea ceremony begins [IMAGE 29-30].

Moon Seen as Exiles
by an anonymous internee

Here in Minidoka in Idaho,
on the high plains with sagebrush,
packs of coyotes roam at night.

[Woman places flat rock on the plate.]

Even though spring comes,
no flowers bloom.
In summer, strong winds whirl,
in winter, snowstorms hit our windows.

[Woman pours sand on the rock.]

Bearing on our backs the word enemy,
we ten thousand, wire-fenced in,
endure a wretched life severed from yesteryear.

[Woman pours water on sand and rock.]

In fifty years of endeavor and work,
we had built a foundation.
Abandoning it, we watch the moon. Exiles.

[Woman piles a round rock on the flat rock.]

Top IMAGE 29: Marsha Paludan as Issei Woman.

Bottom, IMAGE 30: Marsha Paludan as Issei Woman

(All photographs by Roger Shimomura, *Trans-Siberian Excerpts*, February 14-15, 1987, Lawrence Art Center: Lawrence, Kansas).

No matter how hard our pains,
we sacrifice under national policy,
taking each other's hands, vowing to endure.

[Woman pours sand on the round rock.]

When the breeze of peace blows,
Spring with blooming flowers will come around.
Then our pains will become a tale of past dreams.

[Woman pours water on the sand and round rock.] [30]

As the picture slide changes to red, the performer stands, exiting into the darkness. She reappears on the right pedestal and sits for another ceremony; however, for this mock tea ceremony, she is illuminated by a picture slide of the legs of the Jayhawk mascot. Seated across from her at the table is a life-like child puppet dressed in Jayhawks' fan gear and maneuvered by Kurogo 2. The music is a Japanized version of the University of Kansas fight song. In Japanese, Shimomura's parody poem is read:

Here in Lawrence, Kansas,
near farms planted of wheat,
packs of dogs roam at night.

[Woman unwraps folded paper and spreads it on the plate.
Doll moves and gestures, acknowledging this action.]

When spring comes, flowers bloom.
In summer the heat and humidity come.
In winter the snow piles high on our flat-top roofs.

[Woman places flat rock on the plate. Doll stands and watches closely.]

Bearing on our backs the word Jayhawks,
we ten thousand season ticket holders
endure another season in the Big 8.

[Woman places second flat rock on the plate. Doll watches closely.]

In over one hundred years of competition,
we have yet to build a tradition.
Still we come back to watch the team.

[Woman places third flat rock on the plate. Doll steps back.]

No matter how easy the schedule,
we continue to lose,
Taking each other's hands, we vow to continue our support.

[Woman pours red ketchup and yellow mustard onto the rocks on the plate.]

When the end of the season comes, winter will be upon us.
Then our pains will be eased by Larry Brown's basketball team.

[Woman places a fourth flat rock on the plate. Doll sits back down in its chair.] [31]

The music fades, and the woman and doll bow. A kurogo turns the doll's head to the audience in a sarcastic final gesture of ridiculous knowing. The performance ends and fades to black. Shimomura uses the two poems—the first a historical account of a severe tragedy, and the second, a meaningless amusement in sporting—to contrast and highlight events of importance and unimportance in the artist's life. The artist uses the same structure and poetic form in the two segments of the performance, as both poems are read in Japanese, distancing an American audience from their meaning, and giving authentic voice and primacy of importance to the internee's words. Shimomura uses rocks he selected from his own garden in Kansas—rocks that he collects every year during his annual walk along the Washington State beaches. Shimomura plays off the choreographed, austere, aesthetic importance of the Japanese tea ceremony, a thousand-year-old tradition, and replaces the rare and valuable commodity of tea with sand and the fine art vessels with rocks. These ubiquitous objects, sand and rock, are symbolic of the climate internees endured, the lack of resources internees were provided, and the stripping of culture internees faced. In the parody, Shimomura augments the tea ceremony further through a college tailgate party, with ketchup, mustard, and a life-sized puppet of a child to shock the audience through the pageantry and familiarity of the spectacle of college sports.

Junko's Song

Junko Sakurada was a famous Japanese teen pop star in the mid-1970s. Junko's most famous songs were about boy-girl young love—teenage crush songs. She is represented in "Junko's Song" by a performer who stands center stage between the two pedestals, wearing a plaid dress, white gloves, and a non-Kabuki mask with large blue eyes. As the performer lip-syncs the song into a Mr. Microphone, making cute gestures at the audience while bouncing around the stage, she occasionally looks into binoculars. After twenty seconds, pairs of images representing what Junko sees in her binoculars flank the performer, rotating every two seconds until the song is over. Some of the images include Japanese Zero fighter planes, women's high heels, religious crosses, Japanese masks with blue eyes, and Andy Warhol's images of Liz Taylor and Marilyn Monroe. One of the most disturbing images is of a young Asian woman with a gun held to her temple [IMAGE 31]. The stark contrast between Junko's song, appearance, and bubbly gestures and the gruesomeness of what is seen through the binoculars is alarming. Shimomura plays with the power of the Gaze and performativity, as Junko acts kawaii (cute) while internally she is filled with teenage hormones

IMAGE 31: Marsha Paludan as Junko Sakurada (Photograph by Roger Shimomura, *Trans-Siberian Excerpts*, February 14-15, 1987, Lawrence Art Center: Lawrence, Kansas).

and negative thoughts. The audience cannot see inside Junko's mind, but Shimomura uses binoculars to focus on what is in the distance and invisible. While the audience does not know the lyrics of the song, unless they speak Japanese, Shimomura digs beneath the artifice of Japan's kawaii culture and American notions of beauty and stardom to unearth the horrible reality of issues spanning back to World War II and increased Western cultural interaction in Japanese culture, digging into notions of beauty, love and identity.

Playroom

"Playroom" is a four-minute video about cultural interaction, seen through a child's eyes. Shimomura employs his comparative strategy again in "Playroom," juxtaposing the innocence of childhood with the adult, violent realities of racism and stereotypes. Literally referencing a child's playroom, Shimomura employs his dark humor by using a male figure wearing a devil mask who plays with a variety of children's toys. As children are permitted to try on various identities in an attempt to understand who they are, learning their emotions and organizing the world in which they live, the play aspect of "Playroom" is pushed to the extreme by the artist's selection of a devil. The devil performer takes two dissimilar toys and crashes them into each other, forcing them to interact. All of the toys in the playroom come from Shimomura's personal collection, consisting of puzzles, figurines, pin backs (clip badge), coins, and rubber miniatures derived from racist, World War II propaganda to Disney and Marvel comics. In the background, music from a popular children's show in Japan is heard. Shimomura makes a direct and compelling statement about children learning from the examples of their environment and their elders. When Shimomura was incarcerated as a toddler for no reason other than being Japanese American, what was the lesson that he was taught about himself and his family's identity? Shimomura reexamines the meaning of these objects in his life, perhaps playing devil's advocate, to remove the mask of injustice and prejudice that Japanese Americans endured.

Minidoka Girls

Like "Moon Seen as Exiles," "Minidoka Girls" was inspired by a poem written by an anonymous internee at Minidoka. But, unlike "Moon Seen as Exiles," "Minidoka Girls" examines assimilation and identity through the internees'

Top left, IMAGE 32: Detail.

Top right, IMAGE 33: Dan Patrick Lassley as Devil.

Center left, IMAGE 34: Marsha Paludan as Issei.

Center right and bottom left, IMAGES 35 and 36: Details.

(All photographs by Roger Shimomura, *Trans-Siberian Excerpts*, February 14-15, 1987, Lawrence Art Center: Lawrence, Kansas).

IMAGE 37: Joe Reichlin (Photograph by Roger Shimomura, *Trans-Siberian Excerpts*, February 14-15, 1987, Lawrence Art Center: Lawrence, Kansas).

direct environment. Read only in Japanese, the first line of the poem is read, "When we came from afar, to Minidoka by train," as the sound of a train and two picture slides of Japanese American internees lining up to board appear. Internees had no idea that they would be taken to temporary prisons located in harsh, uninhabitable land [IMAGE 32]. The next line is read in Japanese, "Snakes came to see us, shaking their rattles," and the music changes to synthesized crashing and collapsing sounds, and then silence. Shimomura brings in his trademark moments of dark humor—for example, by having a spotlit performer wearing a devil mask shake rattles next to a microphone to simulate rattlesnakes [IMAGES 33-34]. The third and fourth lines, "Minidoka girls need no powder / From the dirt and dust they become white," are accompanied by a performer dressed in a kimono and Noh mask hitting two powder puffs together between two sets of images—Andy Warhol's iconic Elizabeth Taylor and Marilyn Monroe paintings [IMAGES 35-36]. Shimomura is commenting on the whiteness, assimilation, and Americanness that were forced onto Japanese Americans to prove their loyalty and allegiance to the United States. Anything pertaining to Japanese culture—books, clothes, food—was considered suspect and disloyal to the United States during World War II. Shimomura furthers this interpretation with the patriotic music he adds to this moment of the performance. Clearly Minidoka girls were not, nor could they ever be, white, because they were of Japanese ancestry, and while they were American citizens by birth, they were enemies of the U.S. government.

In Japanese, the performer wearing the devil mask states, "Hot! Hot! We came out of the house," and a circular ring is set on fire by the kurogo and then quickly extinguished in a tray of water [IMAGE 37]. The sixth line of the poem, "At the moon the coyotes were howling," and picture slides of the moon and a barracks interior are shown side-by-side. Danger lurked from every possible moment—from rattlesnakes and dust storms to intense heat and coyotes. The poem and performance end with fifteen sets of documentary images of life at Minidoka, while the last two lines are read in

IMAGE 38: Details (Photograph by Roger Shimomura, *Trans-Siberian Excerpts*, February 14-15, 1987, Lawrence Art Center: Lawrence, Kansas).

Japanese: "Don't you know the Minidoka specialties? Snakes, coyotes, and sandstorms" [IMAGE 38].[32]

Shimomura uses popular culture and pop art to make the unknown topic of Japanese American history accessible to an American audience. Andy Warhol is considered by the artist as a significant mentor in his use of popular culture to speak to a broader audience, making fine art accessible to a large segment of the population and setting his own rules while dismantling institutional power. Because the artist chooses to have the poem read in Japanese, just as it was written in Japanese, Shimomura deliberately removed access to the internee's words, just as the United States does not provide equal access for its nonwhite members. Furthermore, Shimomura reveals the rebelliousness of Japanese Americans in maintaining their culture despite being unjustly persecuted, through haiku clubs in which they expressed their feelings in their native tongue. Shimomura recodes this lesser known history through parody and U.S. popular culture. Shimomura incorporates documentary photographs of the Japanese American incarceration and this firsthand account of, presumably, a teenage female internee, to shed a brighter light on the Japanese American incarceration history.

Hymn

According to Shimomura, "Hymn" was the "most complex piece to accomplish because it kept suggesting different directions throughout the writing process, and its content still remains elusive."[33] "Hymn" is an homage to the Japanese American veterans of World War II. This performance piece is about Pearl Harbor, the 442nd all-mainland Japanese American Infantry Regiment, the 100th all-Hawaiian Japanese American Infantry Battalion, and the devastating effects of war. "Hymn" begins with two images of hands making sushi, projected on the left and right side of the stage. In the center sits a *sushiyasan* (sushi chef) who greets a Nisei vet who enters from the

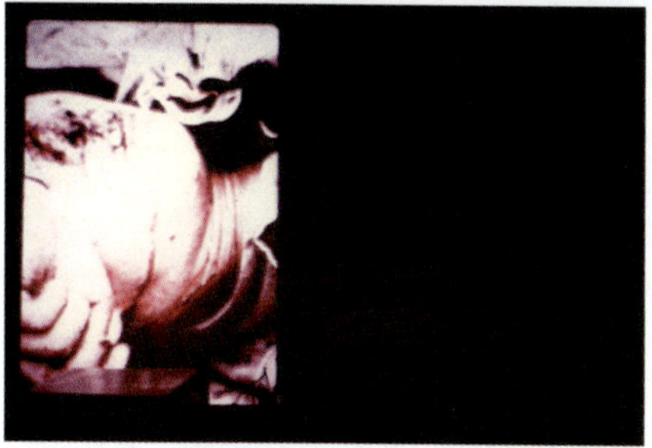

Top, IMAGE 39: Marsha Paludan as Nisei Veteran;
Left, IMAGE 40: Detail; Right, IMAGE 41: Detail.

(All photographs by Roger Shimomura, *Trans-Siberian Excerpts*, February 14-15, 1987, Lawrence Art Center: Lawrence, Kansas).

back of the room and sits on the right side of stage to be served by the sushiyasan. A Hawaiian war chant is heard, followed by a gunshot. After each gunshot, the sushiyasan places an object into a bowl and consecrates the object with an atomizer before placing it on the wall behind the seated Nisei vet [IMAGE 39]. The image of the object is projected on the left side of the stage once it is placed into the sushiyasan's bowl. This sequence is repeated seven more times. The eight objects are a patent leather shoe, a gun, glasses, a clock, a camera, a pineapple, a fan, and a banana. They represent the Nisei veterans of war through direct and indirect associations. For example, the banana is a racial pun for Asian Americans as being yellow on the outside and white on the inside, while the patent leather shoe, gun, and glasses refer directly to soldiers. After the sushiyasan completes placing all eight objects on the wall, the music changes to ominous and violent overtones. The center and right side of the stage fade to black, and the Hawaiian war chant and gunshot begin another cycle of eight, revealing on the left side of the stage eight photographs of mutilated bodies resulting from war, symbolizing the deaths of the eight Nisei soldiers [IMAGE 40]. The 442nd Infantry Regiment and the 100th Infantry Battalion were the most decorated

U.S. military units during World War II, and they also had the highest casualties. After the last photograph, the left side of the stage goes black, and the right side is reilluminated to reveal a Christian cross adorned by the eight objects. Religious organ music plays to complete "Hymn" [IMAGE 41].

Three Haiku

"Three Haiku" was also derived from Toku's diaries and writings and was written by an anonymous internee, but Shimomura reversed their order for this performance piece to symbolize the death of Japanese culture, specifically for Japanese Americans. For Shimomura, reversing the order of the haikus meant rebirth as an "American."[34] As the culmination to *Trans-Siberian Excerpts*, "Three Haiku" delves into the multilayered complexities caused by the Japanese American incarceration through historical, familial/generational, cultural, and political lenses. The irony that the same government that accused all Japanese Americans of being enemies of the state and imprisoned them without just cause because they were of Japanese ancestry would also reconnect a Japanese American son with his Japanese heritage by teaching him how to speak and read Japanese and fight on behalf of the United States in the western theater of the war is part of the absurdity, sarcasm, shock, and parody that Shimomura explores in all the performance pieces of *Trans-Siberian Excerpts*. "Three Haiku" focuses on the tragedy of war and the crimes against humanity that occur when cultural morality is compromised in the name of nationalism.

"Three Haiku" begins with the Japanese character for 'end' appearing on the screen, signifying not only the end of *Trans-Siberian Excerpts* but also the end of the war and those Japanese and Japanese American men, women, and children who lost their lives fighting for freedom and peace. In Japanese, a Japanese voice reads the first haiku, stating, "This is the place where I bury the bones of my son who died in war." The poem refers to any father and son, who died in battle. Poetically, the haiku speaks to the severed connection to history and heritage that immigrants and their families face when moving abroad. A performer dressed in a white kimono as a samurai commits *seppuku* (suicide) [IMAGE 42]. First, the kurogo ties the samurai's headband around the performer's head before he sits down and takes a sip of sake. Shimomura uses picture slides to change the lighting from black, to blue, and then to clear during this scene. Then the samurai unwraps a knife and stabs himself in the stomach, changing the picture slide to red before switching to black [IMAGE 43].

Top, IMAGE 43: Marsha Paludan as man.

Left, IMAGE 42: Marsha Paludan as warrior.

Right, IMAGE 44: Marsha Paludan as Nisei Solider.

(All photographs by Roger Shimomura, *Trans-Siberian Excerpts*, February 14-15, 1987, Lawrence Art Center: Lawrence, Kansas).

Above, IMAGE 45: Marsha Paludan as Nisei Solider.

Left, IMAGE 46: Marsha Paludan as a Young Man.

(All photographs by Roger Shimomura, *Trans-Siberian Excerpts*, February 14-15, 1987, Lawrence Art Center: Lawrence, Kansas).

Spotlit, Kurogo 2 now pulls from the belly of the fallen samurai a bouquet of flowers, taking one flower and placing it in a vase off to the left side of the stage. The samurai rises, changes kimonos, walks up to the flower, and deliberately plucks all the petals off [IMAGE 44]. In Japanese, the second haiku is read: "For twenty years I raised my son to make him an enemy of my country." The internee expresses how futile he or she feels to have invested all of his or her love and energy raising a child who now is seen by the U.S. government as an enemy. This refers to any immigrant raised in a foreign country and is now seen as an enemy of his or her homeland. Shimomura uses the flower as symbolic of the lengthy time required to nurture a plant to flower whose blooms are then so quickly destroyed.

The performer now places a basket on his head and uses a walking stick to become a "disgraced" monk with ukiyo-e images of Japan's landscapes projected onto the background [IMAGE 45]. In Japanese, the audience hears the final haiku: "Drafted by our enemy, my son learned the Japanese language." After the monk walks across the stage, a picture slide of Japanese characters for beginning appears. The monk, symbolic of an exiled and reformed person, changes from kimono to white dinner jacket. Japanese pop and boogie-woogie music begins. He starts dancing, which is described by Shimomura as an "angry young man devilishly dancing," and halfway through his dance, a kurogo brings him an inflatable globe with the Trans-Siberian Railway marked prominently in red [IMAGE 46]. The dancing, acculturated young man throws back the globe to the kurogo, and the dance concludes, as does *Trans-Siberian Excerpts*. Shimomura ends with "Three Haiku" because the journey along the railway is over, paralleling the journey of Japanese Americans. Their connection to Japan is forever broken, and they are assimilated into U.S. culture.

Marsha Paludan as Bon Odori Dancer (Photograph by Roger Shimomura, *Funky Odori,* April 24-25, 1987, Spring Festival, Eastern Illinois University: Charleston, Illinois).

funky odori

- **Grand Ballroom, Eastern Illinois University, Charleston, Illinois, April 24–25, 1987**

Funky Odori is a performance art piece showcasing the reification of cultural authenticity through the dance of Bon Odori. Shimomura describes _Funky Odori_ as similar to the childhood game of telephone, where a message or story is communicated from person to person, resulting in an unrecognizable version of the original. The timeline for _Funky Odori_ begins in 1975, when Shimomura attended his "first authentic 'Bon Odori' (Festival Dance) at the Sanno Festival in Tokyo, Japan [IMAGE 48]."[35] In 1985, Shimomura videotaped the rehearsals of the "Seafair," Seattle's Bon Odori at the Japanese Buddhist Church, where the Issei (first generation) taught the Nisei (second generation), Sansei (third generation) and Yonsei (fourth generation) the six dances to be performed [IMAGE 49]. This tradition has taken place since 1950. In 1986, Shimomura then worked with Marsha Paludan, the choreographer, to memorize one movement from each of the six Bon Odori dances, which were then choreographed into a musical dance piece accompanied by an original musical score composed by Marty Olson based on traditional Japanese folk music that Shimomura provided [IMAGE 50].

In 1987, "How to Do the Funky Odori" was first performed as a short piece in Shimomura's *Trans-Siberian Excerpts* by two dance students, Dan Lassley and Joe Reichlin, to whom Paludan taught the choreographed dance [IMAGE 51]. Three months later, Lassley and Reichlin taught the "Funky Odori" to a group of college students at Eastern Illinois University for their annual "Spring Festival," which Shimomura watched, stating, "The resulting dance I saw didn't even resemble the dance I saw in Tokyo, Japan [IMAGE 52]."[36] The transmission of cultural history over landscapes and across time gradually dissipates when the connection to the authentic source is severed. Shimomura finds this to be the case with the Japanese American experience, resulting from devastating and horrific tragedies caused by World War II.

Top, IMAGE 48: Sanno Festival, (Video still, courtesy of Roger Shimomura, 1975, Tokyo, Japan.

Bottom, IMAGE 49: Seafair, Bon Odori, (Video still, courtesy of Roger Shimomura, 1985, Seattle, Washington).

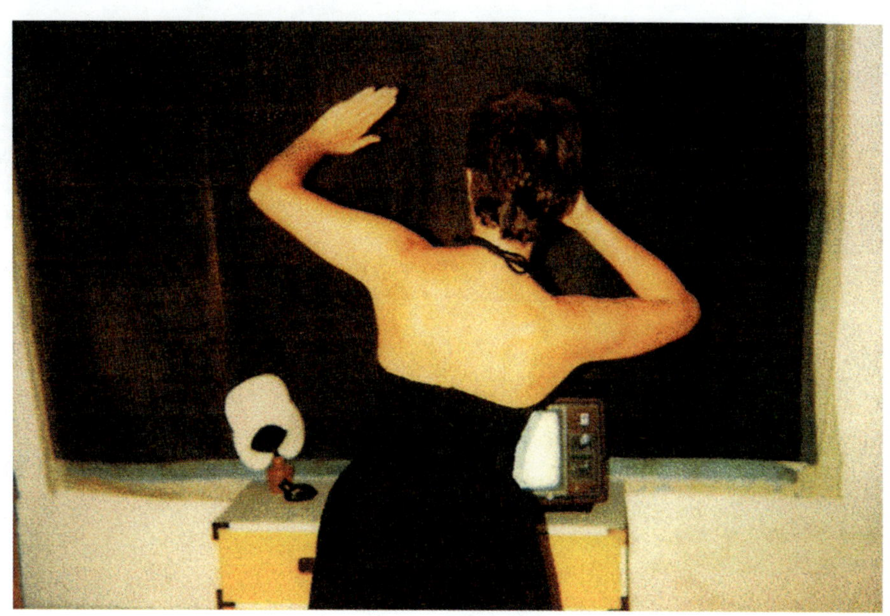

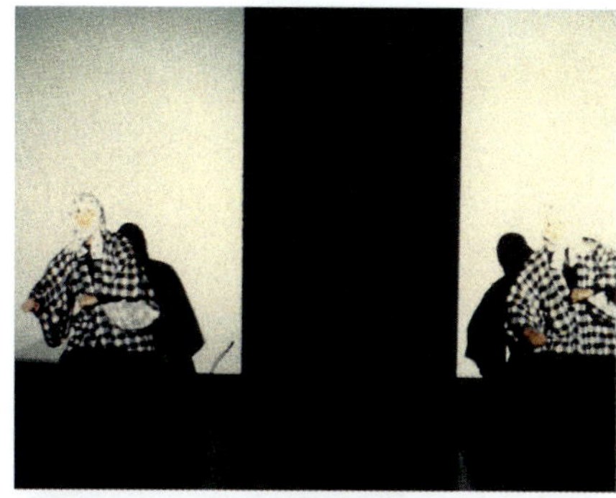

Top, IMAGE 50: Marsha Paludan as Bon Odori Dancer.

Center, IMAGE 51: Dan Lassley and Joe Reichlin as Bon Odori Dancers.

Bottom, IMAGE 52: Student participants from *Funky Odori*.

(Photographs by Roger Shimomura, *Funky Odori*, April 24-25, 1987, Grand Ballroom, Eastern Illinois University: Charleston, Illinois).

Patti Harumoto as Japanese Girl (*California Sushi*, video still, January 10-13, 1990, Franklin Furnace: New York City, New York).

california sushi

5

- "Make Rice, Not War," The Bottleneck, Lawrence, Kansas, December 12, 1988
- "Make Rice, Not War," "Valeda Daze," and "K.I.K.E.," Bernice Steinbaum Gallery, New York City, New York, January 14, 1989
- Cabana Room, Center on Contemporary Art (CoCA), Seattle, Washington, August 4–5, 1989
- Franklin Furnace, New York City, New York, January 10–13, 1990.
- The Maintenance Shop, Iowa State University, Ames, Iowa, March 22, 1990
- "Valeda Daze" and "Better Homes," The Decade Show Performance Series, Studio Museum Harlem, New York City, New York, June 15, 1990

Shimomura creates art about the Nikkei experience because he believes in the tremendous value that can be gleaned. Shimomura's Issei grandmother's diaries directly inspired the artist's first two performance pieces, *Toku's Dance* and *Seven Kabuki Plays Project*. These performances are based on Toku's firsthand account of the Japanese American incarceration and provide insight from the lesser-known perspective of an Issei woman. Shimomura's subsequent performance piece, *Trans-Siberian Excerpts*, was a global and more expansive examination of cultural morality that provided a broader awareness of the effects of repressive governmental structures and a greater sensitivity to cultural differences. Although still informed by Toku's experience and that of Japanese Americans during World War II, Shimomura wrote this piece while traveling along the Trans-Siberian Railway as part of his trip around the world examining cross-cultural interactions. Shimomura's fourth performance, *California Sushi*, shifted the artist's focus to an autobiographical examination of the objects, images, and experiences that informed his life.

California Sushi focuses on post World War II racial and discriminatory issues faced by Asian Americans and personally experienced by Shimomura. An avid collector of material culture from the 1940s and 1950s, ranging from comics, media, Americana, and children's toys to hateful and racially charged propaganda centered around Asian Americans, Shimomura immersed himself in these objects, ordering, reordering, and juxtaposing them until he recreated a level of emotional tension reflective of memories throughout the artist's life. More specifically, these emotionally charged memories speak to a lack of societal compassion and a lack of awareness of cultural differences. While the notion of cultural mixing and appropriation is evident in the title of the performance piece, *California Sushi*, which refers to Japanese American culture adapting Japanese cuisine to its geography, available food resources, and consumer-culture tastes, Shimomura critically examines the cultural combinations, describing the effects as forming "generalities and social aberrations within one's own ethnic family."[37] In this way, Shimomura's work operates to investigate and analyze the Japanese American experience from within.

California Sushi is a collection of seven short performances that use the same format: a performer and a kurogo, and a stage divided by side-by-side projections using a video monitor (left) and picture slides (right). The entire suite of performances is bookended by an opening and closing video that topically introduces the significant symbolism within the artist's life. The University of Kansas, General Research Grant, and the National Endowment of the Arts, Art Matters Inc., provided funding for this project.

Opening Video

Theater doors are opened, allowing the audience to take their seats while a video plays at the front of the theater; it depicts a young Asian girl, dressed in Western attire, carrying a Mickey Mouse doll, an electric rice cooker, a large mallet, and a World War II model U.S. fighter airplane. The girl is seen far off in the distance down an endless country dirt road. Her identity and the symbolic objects she holds are unrecognizable [IMAGE 54]. Over five minutes, the girl approaches the camera until she is in close-up, and her identity as well as the objects she holds is visible to the audience, before the video fades to black. During the course of the video, an a cappella version of one of the Chinese American musician Yo-Yo Ma's cello sonatas is heard. Shimomura uses the opening video to not only provide an introduction to the cultural mixing that he addresses in *California Sushi* but also the most significant symbolic objects in his oeuvre.

IMAGE 54: Patti Harumoto as Japanese Girl (Video still, *California Sushi,* January 10-13, 1990, Franklin Furnace: New York City, New York).

Shimomura carefully orchestrates the symbolism in the opening video. Yo-Yo Ma is perhaps the most famous Asian American and is symbolic of the success of acculturation to Western society; Ma is symbolic of the model minority myth.[38] The Asian girl, along with the objects she carries, functions as a constellation of meaning that Shimomura regularly employs in his paintings and performance art. Her American citizenship is unclear. She is young and innocent, and she greets the audience with a smile while holding a Mickey Mouse doll, and yet she also carries a weapon (mallet) and a U.S. warplane. She is dressed in 1950s attire but also carries an electric rice cooker as a symbol of the modern Asian American experience. She is a consumer of American culture and placed in the U.S. countryside, but it is unknown why she is here and what she intends to do with the objects that she clutches in her arms. Shimomura welcomes the audience to *California Sushi* through these popular-culture icons that are teeming with metaphoric meaning.

Make Rice, Not War

The first performance, "Make Rice, Not War," begins with a darkened room and the sound of the iconic "The Stars and Stripes Forever" march composed

IMAGES 55 and 56: Tony Allard as Solider (Photograph by Roger Shimomura, *California Sushi*, January 10-13, 1990, Franklin Furnace: New York City, New York).

by John Philip Sousa, a U.S. Marine Band leader from 1880 to 1892.[39] A spotlight illuminates a highly decorated U.S. solider, presumably a high-ranking general or commanding officer. In his cupped hands, he carries plastic toy soldiers and wears Asian eyeglasses [IMAGE 55]. As he moves across the stage, his movements are modeled after *Noh* dance.[40] Once reaching a table with an electric rice cooker, the solider uses ceremonial gestures with militaristic precision to wash the rice, pour the clean rice, water, and toy soldiers into the cooker, place the lid on top, and turn the cooker on [IMAGE 56]. Before the soldier exits, he performs a military salute, bows, and walks off stage in a Noh-esque style, to the conclusion of "The Stars and Stripes Forever."

The title, "Make Rice, Not War," is a pun on the slogans of the late 1960s antiwar movements, "Make love, not war." However, Shimomura layers the 1896 classic patriotic "The Stars and Stripes Forever" march with a U.S. soldier, Japanese Noh-style movement, childhood toys, a modern electric rice cooker, and yellow-face eyeglasses to create a cross-culturally and cross-generationally inspired performance about cultural understanding and, most importantly, peace. By making an Asian staple food instead of going into battle, Shimomura comments on the basic human needs of survival in lieu of war. The United States was heavily engaged in wars throughout the

Pacific Ocean with Asian countries, including Japan, Korea, Vietnam, and China. These wars not only affected public perception of Asians and Asian Americans as Others, but they also altered the demographics of the United States through an influx of refugees and immigrants.

On a personal level, Shimomura was referencing the Japanese American Nisei fighters of World War II, who were unjustly imprisoned and then permitted to fight on behalf of the United States, but only in the European arena, and who distinguished themselves as the most highly decorated battalion in that war. In 1988, President Ronald Reagan signed the Civil Liberties Act of 1988 (Redress Act) as a symbolic governmental gesture to acknowledge the unlawful actions of the U.S. government.[41] While Shimomura uses parody to bring attention to this topic and elicit peace over war, his intention is not to offend decent Americans.[42] Shimomura is proud to be a U.S. citizen. Like many of his fellow Nisei citizens, Shimomura enlisted and served in the U.S. military, in his case from 1962–1964, as part of his civic duty.

Valeda Daze

"Valeda Daze" refers to a Japanese American Greek sorority at the University of Washington, Shimomura's undergraduate institution. The performance begins on the video monitor with a close-up of the title page for "Valeda" (meaning "wise woman") in Shimomura's 1961 yearbook and then fades to black. In the darkness, a male voice is heard repeating, "One, two, cha-cha-cha," several times before the TV monitor fades in, depicting a long shot of the same Valeda title page. As the camera slowly moves over the page during the next ninety seconds, zooming in on individual members' faces and then back out, Frankie Avalon's song "Venus" plays. At thirty seconds into the video, a yellow picture slide appears on the right side of the monitor, highlighting a male performer wearing a mask of Shimomura at age eighteen and dancing the chalypso, referring to the Afro-Cuban music that revived the traditional Cuban "cha-cha" dance, popular in the 1950s [IMAGE 57]. After approximately ninety seconds, a female voice reads the mission statement of the Valeda organization as the video, dancing, and music continue:

> *Valeda is a campus group that was organized in 1947 to promote friendship and scholarship among the Nisei women, as well as to have social and service activities. This group is composed mainly of Japanese girls but open to all who wish to join. After serving a*

IMAGE 57: Tony Allard as Young Roger (Photograph by Roger Shimomura, *California Sushi*, January 10-13, 1990, Franklin Furnace: New York City, New York).

> *quarter as a pledge, during which time the genuineness of her desire to be a working member of the group is tested, a Valeda helps to get new freshmen acquainted with college life. She also provides the help to the university in such programs as Parent's Weekend and, with special emphasis on service to the Japanese community, helps in charity work and in projects like working on the community float.*

Valeda is a Greek word meaning "wise woman," and the club wants to develop in its members those qualities that befit a wise woman. It inspires its members to scholastic achievement, helps maintain a sense of social responsibility, and helps members form many valuable and lasting friendships.[43]

After an extreme close-up on a single Valeda member, the video and Avalon's "Venus" simultaneously end, fading to black. In the darkness, a male voice is heard again, repeating, "One, two, cha-cha-cha." The video monitor fades in and features an Asian girl dancing with a seven-foot-tall inflatable Superman doll to Sonny James's "Young Love." After approximately fifteen seconds, the doll's air valve is opened, deflating the Superman doll over the next ninety seconds as the couple continues to awkwardly dance. After approximately ninety seconds, a blue picture slide is projected on the right side of the TV monitor, and the male performer, wearing a mask depicting Shimomura at age forty-nine, resumes dancing the chalypso, although this time he is out of rhythm with James's "Young Love" [IMAGE 58]. The entire performance comes to an end when Superman is completely deflated, and the video monitor and performer fade to black.

IMAGE 58: Tony Allard as Middle-age Roger (Photograph by Roger Shimomura, *California Sushi*, January 10-13, 1990, Franklin Furnace: New York City, New York).

Shimomura calls attention to the irony of the Valeda sorority being for Nisei women to "adapt" to college life, foster "social" responsibility, and provide service to the "Japanese community." Although Valeda opens membership to all who wish to join, the need for this segregated sorority raises questions about the lack of cultural understanding of differences that is present in the college's Greek system. Founded in 1947, this sorority was established four years after the end of Japanese American incarceration and World War II, three years prior to the lifting of immigration quotas and citizenship restrictions in the United States, and eighteen years prior to the banning of antimiscegenation laws (outlawing interracial marriage). Shimomura adds his own awkward exposure to cultural mixing through dancing the chalypso (an Afro-Cuban dance), to a popular 1950s song encapsulating the naiveté of young idyllic love and not being bound by social constraints of religion, class, race, and gender to this history. Shimomura highlights the power of these societal factors that cause the older Shimomura, more socially engrained and set in his ways, to dance less successfully to the beat of the music. Paired with the video of the Asian girl dancing with the deflating Superman doll, Shimomura parodies a failed social coupling. In several of his other works, Shimomura uses Superman—an iconic comic book character sent from another planet—as an ironic symbol of the U.S. government's actions toward Japanese Americans, to protect and save Earth people in need. In "Valeda Daze," Shimomura renders Superman helpless and full of hot air, referring to the Greek system within the institutional structure of colleges and more broadly, to societal structures that perpetuate a lack of understanding toward cultural differences.[44] Shimomura shines a critical light on these institutional and socially accepted practices but does not discount the efforts of the Valeda organization.

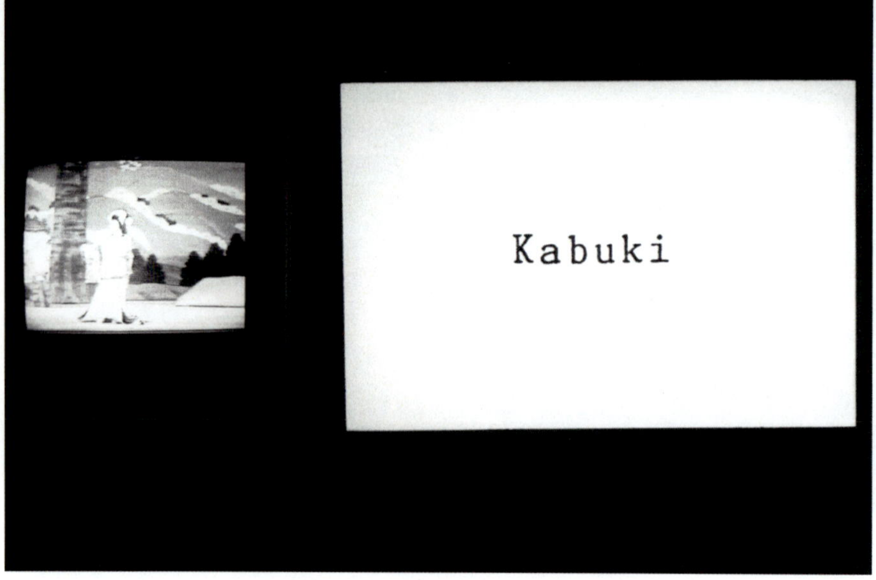

IMAGE 59, Detail (Photograph by Roger Shimomura, *California Sushi*, January 10-13, 1990, Franklin Furnace: New York City, New York).

K.I.K.E.

Using the thread of ironic humor, Shimomura's "K.I.K.E." (kinky immature kimono empress)" is a performance piece about cultural sensitivity, stereotypes, and racism. Through reversal of the acronym, the artist turns the term *kike* into a pun based on the term J.A.P. (Jewish American princess). The seemingly innocuous acronym, J.A.P., carries a negative racial history when referring to someone of Japanese ancestry as a "Jap." Similarly, the term *kike* is racist slang for someone of Jewish heritage. The origins of this performance were inspired by a direct conversation Shimomura had at a faculty party at the University of Kansas. Shimomura created the piece to point to the absurdity of sociocultural logic that belittles or makes light of racial slurs and hate speech, even if accidental in origin, unintentional, or behind closed doors. Using stereotypical language is a form of name-calling and belittling that speaks for and defines another without his or her permission. While seemingly a small act, when taken to the extreme, it is an act of power, control, and ownership that can lead to more harmful and consequential actions of violence, injustice, and hate.

In a darkened room, background noise of a lively party begins. Over the party noise, a casual conversation between Shimomura and a female professor is heard, first with a greeting and "How are you?" Then the woman says she has a joke for the artist: "Do you know what a JAP [sic] is?" Shimomura is startled and confused, and she repeats herself. Shimomura is offended and asks if she is kidding. After a moment of thought, she says, "Oh my God. I'm sorry. I mean, it's a Jewish American princess..." Shimomura, still confused, ends the conversation by responding, "It's a what?" A video image

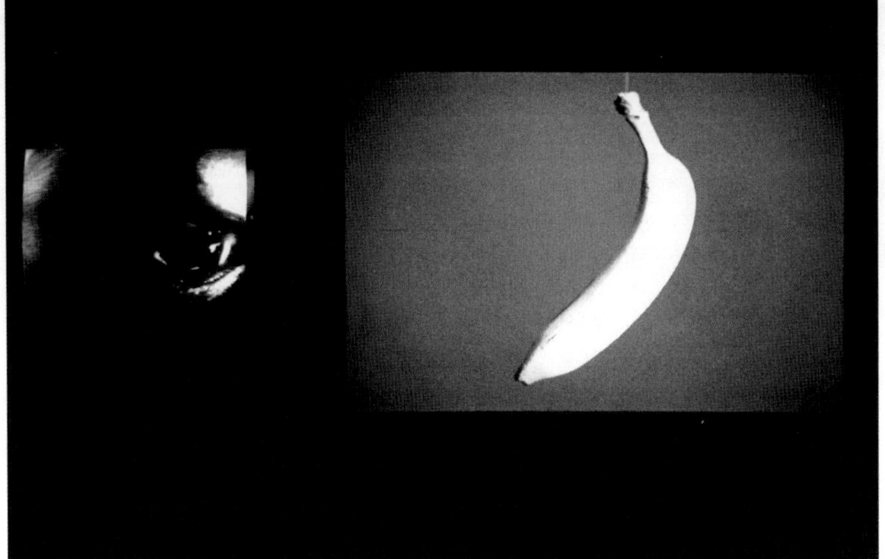

IMAGE 60, Detail (Photograph by Roger Shimomura, *California Sushi*, January 10-13, 1990, Franklin Furnace: New York City, New York).

of a Kabuki dancer appears on the monitor on the left, and simultaneously, a picture slide of the word *Kabuki* appears on the right for five seconds [IMAGE 59]. The video image then goes black, while a clacking sound introduces the next word, *Imperial*, which is shown for five seconds, followed by clack, *Kendo*, clack, and *Empire* on the slide projector as the background party sounds continue. The words repeat the sequence, K., I., K., E., before starting again with a new series of words—"Karate, Ikebana, Kyoto, Eastern; Kamikaze, Ichiban, Katakana, Edo"—with the underlined words indicating a corresponding image shown on the monitor: "Kakemono, Incorrigible, Knowledge, Ebi; Koto, Impeccable, Keen, Elegance; Kill, Ideal, Karma, Exquisite; Keystone, Immigrant, Kick Off, Emigrant; Keeper, Impression, Keystone, English; Kiss, Incompatible, Kowtow, Enemy; Kidnap, Incarcerate, Kangaroo court, Evacuation; Knockers, Inferior, Knockout, Ethnic; Kewpie, Impotent, Knucklehead, Eyeful." When the thirteenth row of K.I.K.E. words is shown, a close-up of an Asian face appears on the monitor, while the picture slides continue, now at an accelerated pace, with a clacking sound introducing each word: "Kiss ass, (banana), Immature, (banana), Kimono, (banana), Empress, (banana), Kiss ass, Immature, Kimono, Empress, K., I., K., E., K.I.K.E" [IMAGE 60]. After the last picture slide is shown, and the close-up video of the Asian face ends, the room goes black.

Shimomura's semiotic image-and-word play for the racist slang *kike* combines humor, sadness, nonsense, and reality in a vein similar to stereotyping, to recode a new narrative of meaning behind the term. Shimomura also alludes to the racial history and social injustice of Japanese and Jewish immigrants during World War II as two targeted and incarcerated populations, although the scale and genocide that people of Jewish heritage experienced is incomparable. The success of Shimomura's performance piece is its failure to convince his audience that the racial slur *kike* means anything other than a form of hate speech for persons of Jewish ancestry, paralleling Shimomura's feeling that *jap* cannot mean anything other than a racist slang for someone of Japanese ancestry.

Shimomura first performed this piece at the Bernice Steinbaum Gallery in New York to an audience before the opening sale of his most recent body of paintings. This was the first time in Shimomura's career that his performance work was shown in a fine art institution. Overall, "K.I.K.E." was received and understood as a critique of all racial stereotypes. Shimomura acknowledges that it did result in one cancellation of the sale of a presold painting, demonstrating the risk the artist encounters when tackling these topics as well as the deep hurt and harm caused by racism, even in the face of understanding.

Tai-Pan Cappy

"Tai-Pan Cappy" is a video mock-interview set in Japan between an American female reporter who speaks fluent Japanese and an American male professor, "Tai-Pan Cappy," who responds primarily in *katakana*, or Japanese syllabary adapted for Western words. Shimomura uses the term *Tai-Pan Cappy*, which originated in the nineteenth century and refers to an egotistical, culturally insensitive, senior business executive working in Asia, as a metaphor for Americans who travel abroad but do not immerse themselves in the foreign culture to which they travel. Instead, these tourists stay in their cultural bubble and patronize only familiar American things. Shimomura deliberately draws on the imperialist and colonial references of this term to delve deeper into the historical contexts that point to the origins of attitudes between colonizer and colonized nations.

As the video opens to Japanese music, the interviewer begins her introduction in Japanese, translated as the following:

> *Professor Hurst, you are the director of the Center for East Asian Studies at the University of Kansas where you are also professor of history; however, you have lived here in Japan for ten of the twenty years you have taught there. During that time you have probably experienced some of the finest cuisine that Japan offers. Can you share with us some of those places that you have eaten?*[45]

IMAGE 61: Cappy Hurst as Tai-pan Cappy (Photograph by Roger Shimomura, *California Sushi*, photograph, January 10-13, 1990, Franklin Furnace: New York City, New York).

Tai-Pan Cappy—Professor Hurst—is a Japanese cultural "expert," living half of the year in Japan for the last twenty years. As the interviewer continues her line of questioning, inquiring about the best Japanese entertainment, hotels, television shows, and movies from this person whom she believes is a cultural insider, each of Tai-Pan Cappy's responses reflect his proximity to U.S. culture and provide no insight into Japanese culture. For example, Professor Hurst's response to the first question states, "Well, actually I have never really taken to Japanese food. I usually eat breakfast at McDonald's, lunch at Shakey's Pizza, and dinner at Kentucky Fried Chicken—or breakfast at Mr. Donut, lunch at Burger King, and dinner at Pizza Hut." Because, Tai-Pan Cappy answers mainly in katakana, which phonetically sounds similar enough to English that a non-Japanese speaker would almost immediately recognize the Japanese word, Shimomura further symbolizes Tai-Pan Cappy's uselessness as a Japanese cultural resource. The entire interview parodies the lack of understanding of cultural difference.

To exacerbate the colonizer mentality, Shimomura includes a Japanese woman who sits to the left of the professor, whose sole responsibility is to shell peanuts and pour sake for the professor during the course of the interview [IMAGE 61]. She is deliberately not given a voice and is placed in a subservient role, despite likely having all of the answers to the interviewer's questions. Shimomura adds her to the interview as another symbolic layer of Tai-Pan Cappy's lack of culture appreciation and respect; he bears no real interest in Japanese culture or in fostering a deeper level of understanding of Japan. In this way, he personifies imperialism.

Despite his profession and geographic accessibility to Japanese culture, Tai-Pan Cappy is a cultural tourist, having made no effort to experience Japan's current culture, describing everything he likes about Japan through the filter of the United States. Eventually, the interviewer drops her head in complete disgust, ending the interview. Professor Hurst, completely unaware of the interviewer's disgust, continues talking. Shimomura created "Tai-Pan Cappy" to highlight the value of interfacing with multiple cultures and to challenge the hegemonic, white, male, Western narrative's supreme importance.

Haiku Rap (Musical Interlude)

Tony Allard composed "Haiku Rap"[46] as an audio intermission for *California Sushi*. Using Japanese and English words, Allard blends familiar U.S. words and melodies with Japanese words to create an awkward cross-cultural song. Allard blends sounds, such as gongs, chimes, and drums, using a synthesizer to create a funky, original beat. Allard was influenced by U.S. rap music and the poetic structure of haiku to create this hybrid composition. The piece is fifty-eight seconds in length.

He

"He" is the most autobiographical piece in *California Sushi*, as the narrated diary entries reflect formative events in Shimomura's life and correlate directly with the video of symbolic objects that Shimomura uses repeatedly in his art. The format of the piece uses a video of an Asian girl interacting with symbolic objects and a spotlit performer, dressed in a samurai mask, pinstripe suit, and Superman undershirt, who reads in a distorted voice from a book describing events from Shimomura's life. The audience interprets the juxtaposition of the narrative read by the masked performer and the choreographed video of an Asian female interacting with significant symbolic objects from the artist's life.

The video opens with an Asian woman putting on makeup in front of a mirror to Japanese melodies performed by Yo-Yo Ma [IMAGE 62]. The background music is heard throughout the entire video. As the video continues, it shows her putting on a Western-style dress as the masked narrator, spotlit next to the video screen, reads the first entry in a distorted voice [IMAGE 63]:

In 1975 he lived in Japan for three months and saw Junko Sakurada on TV. From that moment on, he became fascinated with top-ten shows. He started buying top-ten videos from Uwajimaya's in Seattle, brought them back to Kansas, and watched them for hours. He played them for his friends, but they didn't share in his enthusiasm.[47]

The journal entry contradicts the video performance, as Shimomura was obsessed with a Japanese popular-culture fad known as *kawaii* (cute) that idealized young, innocent, sweet girlishness. But the video portrays an Asian female dressing in Western clothes [IMAGE 64]. Shimomura comments on two cross-cultural interests, with the diary entry reflecting his Japanese ancestry and time in Japan where he developed an obsession with kawaii culture and the video reflecting his U.S. citizenship and interest in being an American.

As the video continues, it shows the Asian woman putting on a blond wig, and the masked performer reads the second entry:

One day his mother gave him all of the drawings that he did in grade school. When he looked at them carefully, he discovered that he

IMAGE 62: Keiko Kira as Asian Woman (Photograph by Roger Shimomura, *California Sushi*, January 10-13, 1990, Franklin Furnace: New York City, New York).

Left, IMAGE 63: Tony Allard as Narrator; above, IMAGE 64: Keiko Kira as Asian Woman (Photographs by Roger Shimomura, *California Sushi*, January 10-13, 1990, Franklin Furnace: New York City, New York).

> *always drew his mother with blond hair. Mrs. Hines, his first-grade teacher, never corrected him but always put a smiling face on his drawings.*[48]

Shimomura addresses his confusion over his removal of his Japanese ancestry from his drawing, as his mother's black hair was made blond. The need for Japanese Americans to assimilate into U.S. culture was paramount over his Japanese ancestry during Shimomura's childhood—so much so that no adult ever questioned his mother's portrait [IMAGE 65]. The video shows the blond-haired, Asian female in a Western dress putting on patent leather shoes [IMAGE 66], and the third entry is read:

> *John, the middle son of a famous painter [Paul Horiuchi], was his best friend but he was Catholic. John told him what movies he couldn't see, what days he had to eat fish, and what penance he had to pay. But most of all, he remembered that John said that good Catholic girls were not supposed to wear patent leather shoes.*[49]

The narrative shifts to highlight Shimomura's awareness of sociocultural rules of acceptable behavior that he recalls from childhood. Although the woman is not abiding by or unaware of these rules, Shimomura creates tension over her character as rebellious in nature versus conforming to social norms. The power of objects as meaningless as a pair of shoes to alter the opinion of others is deeply important to Shimomura's work as a Sansei pop artist. Because these objects appear often in Shimomura's work as important signifiers of meaning, and Shimomura offers clues to their importance in his life, former interpretations of his work take on new meaning.

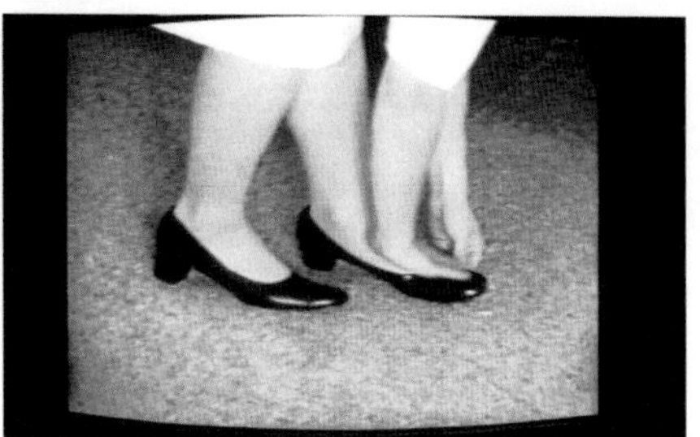

Left, IMAGE 65: Keiko Kira as Asian Woman; right, IMAGE 66: Detail (Photographs by Roger Shimomura, *California Sushi*, January 10-13, 1990, Franklin Furnace: New York City, New York).

As the video resumes, the woman completes her attire by putting on white gloves as the fourth entry is read:

> *He faced the draft after college. Shiro, a famous Nisei vet, said that it was his obligation to become an officer. So when he went into the service, he wore white gloves during inspections. While he hated the army, he loved the parades. He organized his post's honor guard when President Kennedy was assassinated.*[50]

The white gloves are symbolic of Western culture, civilization, and Shimomura's military service. The gloves identify the performative nature and pageantry of "He" and foreshadow the inspection of objects and symbolism in Shimomura's work. The narrative gives greater insight into the military service of Japanese Americans, including Shimomura's own fulfillment of civic duty and service to his country.

As the video continues, the Asian woman, with white gloves and patent leather shoes, and wearing a blond wig and Western dress, picks up a model airplane while the masked narrator reads the fifth entry:

> *He has always loved to draw airplanes. He drew them in Minidoka, in Coleman Grade School, at Washington Junior High, at Garfield High School, at the University of Washington, at Syracuse University, and [he] still draws them in Lawrence, Kansas.*[51]

Shimomura outlines the places and educational institutions that have marked his life through his constant love of drawing airplanes. While the various airplane models reference nations, technology, and tools of war in much of Shimomura's work, they also carry a more innocent, personal meaning as a first childhood love through the diary reading.

The video shows the woman setting down the airplane and picking up a gun while the masked narrator reads the sixth entry:

> *In high school his friend Melvin made a zip gun out of a Gene Autry cap pistol. The first time he shot it, he burnt himself badly. The second time, he shot a robin in his backyard. The third time, he shot his sister's cat by accident. The fourth time he threatened to shoot some students from West Seattle. He was with Melvin all four times.*[52]

Shifting to a serious and violent symbol, a gun, Shimomura further illustrates how memories are tied to objects, and how objects convey meaning. Here, the artist narrates what begins as seemingly innocent childhood play that quickly escalates to the deaths of small animals and threats to fellow students. Guns are not toys; they are weapons and tools with deadly consequences. Shimomura and Melvin quickly learned this lesson [IMAGE 67].

The woman places the gun back and picks up a Bruce Lee puppet as the masked narrator reads the seventh diary entry:

> *He knew Bruce Lee while in college. Bruce was obnoxious and was always doing tricks during lunchtime in the Union. When he went into the army, he received two letters from friends that said his girlfriend was spending a lot of time with Bruce. Ten years later in a bar, his ex-girlfriend told him that Bruce was impotent.*[53]

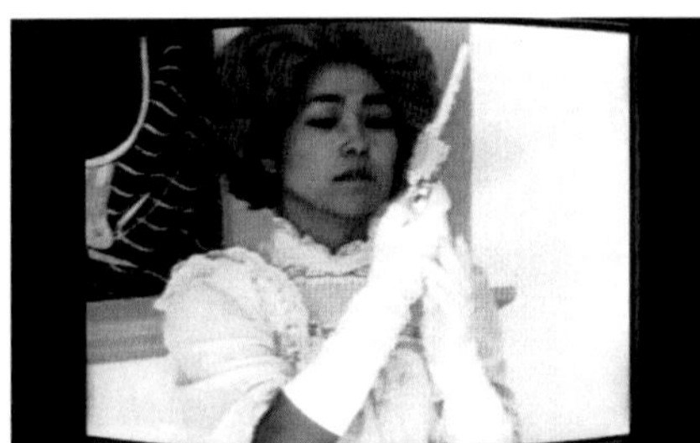

IMAGE 67 and 68: Keiko Kira as Asian Woman; (Photographs by Roger Shimomura, *California Sushi*, January 10-13, 1990, Franklin Furnace: New York City, New York).

Bruce Lee was a famous martial artist and movie star of tremendous talent. While popular culture creates a star image of Lee as superhuman, mythically powerful, and charismatic, Shimomura describes an alternative interpretation based on personal experience that characterizes Lee as obnoxious and impotent. The popular-culture apparatus is an iconographic system about which Shimomura is deeply inquisitive in his work.

The video shows the woman picking up a Mickey Mouse doll while the eighth diary entry is read [IMAGE 68]:

> *He has many drawings of Mickey Mouse that he did in grade school. For twenty years he has used Mickey Mouse in his paintings. He has a big collection of Mickey Mouse toys. He loved Mickey Mouse. Now he is waiting for Walt Disney to sue him.*[54]

Similar to his long-held affinity for airplanes, Shimomura reveals his personal feelings—and a bit of humor—in his attachment to and affection for Mickey Mouse. As a pop artist, Shimomura uses iconic characters such as Mickey Mouse, Superman, Astro Boy, and Pokémon, as national and even global cultural symbols of U.S. and Japanese derivation in his artwork.

The video continues and shows the woman placing Mickey Mouse down on the table and picking up hubcaps as the masked narrator reads the ninth diary entry:

> *While in high school, he was always attracted to hubcaps. Though his grandmother always advised him that "whatever you do, good or bad, will be a reflection on the entire Japanese race," he ignored her advice.*

From the narrative, Shimomura allowed his desire to steal hubcaps that often fell off cars and ended up on the side of the road to overpower his grandmother's warning of negative consequences extending beyond himself. Shimomura maintains a strong desire to collect objects, although now legally.

Now the woman picks up a paintbrush, while the masked narrator reads the tenth diary entry:

His father wanted him to become a doctor. He wanted to be an artist. His father said that dentistry would be a good compromise. But he had his own way. His parents remained skeptical but were thrilled when he became a professor.[55]

Even without his father's implicit support of becoming an artist, Shimomura followed his passion and eventually gained his parents' approval when he became a professor of art.

The woman picks up each object, one by one, and looks at herself in the mirror. Then she exits off-camera before the video fades to black. This final sequence provides the audience an opportunity to mirror the female performer and recall the memories Shimomura described and the meaning ascribed to each object. "He" is directly connected to Shimomura's artistic style as a Sansei pop artist, which juxtaposes Japanese and American popular culture to express his experience as a Japanese American.

Better Homes

"Better Homes" takes its name from *Better Homes and Gardens*, a favorite magazine, that Shimomura's parents would read about U.S. popular values and tastes during the 1940s and 1950s. The content of this magazine contrasts with the content of the performance piece that focuses on a highly descriptive and emotional account of the Japanese American incarceration. Shimomura uses a pop-culture classic horror film to parallel the unreal and devastating experience of the Japanese American incarceration.

"Better Homes" begins with a song segment and video from *Little Shop of Horrors* to introduce, symbolize, and parallel the horrific nature and surreal experience of the Japanese American incarceration [IMAGE 69]. Upon completion of the song, the monitor goes black, and a picture slide of a barbed wire fence appears along with a performer wearing a Hawaiian shirt, an incarceration tag with an identification number, and a basket over his head. He slowly walks across the stage, banging a drum, while three stanzas of "Bugle Song" are heard in Japanese (see below for a translation of "Bugle Song") [IMAGE 70]. Once the performer exits the front of the stage, the picture slide goes to black. However, the beating of the drum continues until the performer again appears, this time walking through the audience as picture slides of the Japanese American incarceration and pages from

Toku Shimomura's diaries during incarceration are shown, alternating every five seconds, for approximately five minutes.

Shimomura creates his own musical time warp, although none of the audience members are invited to join in the tragic narrative. During the drumming performance and picture slides, the first three stanzas of "Bugle Song" are now translated to English and read out loud. The title, "Bugle Song," refers to a simplified brass instrument commonly used as a military call to arms. Toku's book is filled with incarceration poems to Japanese folk melodies, like "Bugle Song," written in Japanese and expressing the anger and outrage felt by the Issei regarding their incarceration [IMAGES 71-72]. These haiku poems were sung at private gatherings to the tunes of Japanese folk melodies. The irony of the song's title, as a Western instrument calling to arms unjustly imprisoned persons of Japanese heritage, is the exact type of contradiction and tension that Shimomura creates in his art.

The remaining sixteen stanzas of the "Bugle Song" (nineteen total) are also sung in English while the drumming performance and picture slides

Left, IMAGE 69: Ellen Greene, *Little Shop of Horrors*, distributed by Warner Bros. 1986; right, IMAGE 70: Tony Allard as Monk (Video still and photograph by Roger Shimomura, *California Sushi*, January 10-13, 1990, Franklin Furnace: New York City, New York).

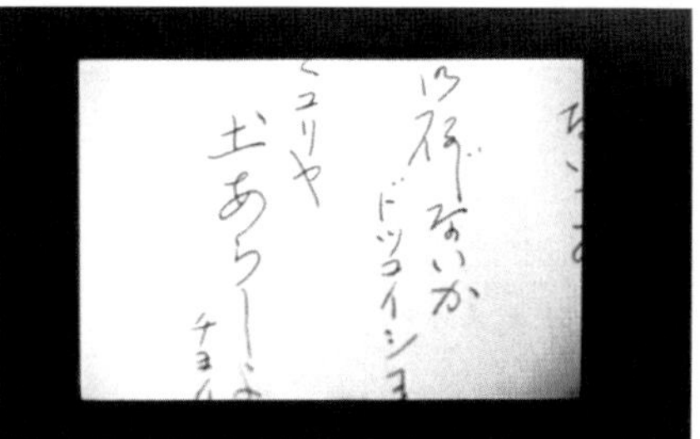

Left and right, IMAGE 71 and 72: Details (Photographs by Roger Shimomura, *California Sushi*, January 10-13, 1990, Franklin Furnace: New York City, New York).

IMAGE 73: Detail (Photograph by Roger Shimomura, *California Sushi*, January 10-13, 1990, Franklin Furnace: New York City, New York).

continue. Once the song is completed, the picture slides and drumming end before a video segment of "Guilty by Reason of Race,"[56] part of the *NBC Report* series, is shown. This was the second major network documentary on the unjust wartime removal and incarceration of Japanese Americans. As the title points out, Japanese Americans were incarcerated for no other reason than their race. However, Shimomura dubs the documentary to the "Little Shop of Horrors" soundtrack, using the same song as before, and he adds a large smiley-face image that a kurogo moves back and forth in front of the video monitor, partially obscuring the screen until the song ends and the entire performance fades to black [IMAGE 73]. Shimomura uses the smiley face to cover up this traumatic past. "Better Homes" is a direct commentary on racism and the injustice of incarceration. It is as scary as a flesh-eating plant out of a work of horror, or science fiction, or comedy.

Bugle Song

1. *Thousands of miles far away from our country,*
   Here is Minidoka, Idaho,
   The name of which I do not know.
   The red sunset is glowing upon us.

2. *When we talk together about our past,*
When we think about the distant future,
Our firm resolution crumbles down,
And I start weeping with my friends.

3. *I wondered if this was just a nightmare, and I worried.*
The dark cloud between Japan and America
On the early morning of December 7th
Became a storm and broke up.

4. *I calmed down my disturbed heart.*
From today on, utterly different from yesterday,
We will be their enemies.
I wonder what will be our end.

5. *I entrusted everything to God,*
Thus making a firm resolution.
But listening to the news, which changed from minute to minute,
Was the only thing I could do.

6. *During the morning,*
Our friends well known to the leaders,
The cloud of suspicion was cast,
And they were caught like criminals.

7. *To their wives and children,*
Not a word were they allowed to say.
On some wrists handcuffs were put,
And they were driven away to an unknown place.

8. *Days passed in anxiety.*
The police pressed on day after day.
With strict restriction,
We followed them and spent days in tears.

9. *Finally it was decided that we should move.*
The solid foundation we built
Over long years was destroyed.
We were sent to the internment camp.

Top left, IMAGE 74: Detail; top right, IMAGE 75: Detail; bottom right, IMAGE 76: Detail.

(All photographs by Roger Shimomura, *California Sushi*, January 10-13, 1990, Franklin Furnace: New York City, New York).

an image of Japan's flag appears on the left monitor, along with a voice with a Japanese accent saying, "This is Japanese." Next, China's flag is projected onto the right screen, along with a voice with a Chinese accent saying, "This is Chinese." Then the video and picture slide return to yellow [IMAGE 74]. Shimomura continues with this visual format, and prior to each comparison a gong is heard to call the audience's attention to the next comparison.

The next comparison begins with Emperor Hirohito's image appearing on the monitor, along with a voice with a Japanese accent stating, "This is Hirohito." The voice with the Chinese accent states, "Hirohito is not Chinese," and a picture slide stating, "NOT CHINESE," appears on the right, while the video changes to yellow, and then the picture slide changes to yellow [IMAGE 75]. Mao Tse-tung's image appears on the screen, and a voice with a Chinese accent states, "This is Mao Tse-tung." The voice with a Japanese accent states, "Mao Tse-tung is not Japanese" [IMAGE 76]. A picture slide stating, "NOT JAPANESE," appears, and then changes to yellow before the sequence continues for six more comparisons, with a gong signaling each new comparison: "Sushi/Dim Sum," "Toshiro Mifune/Bruce Lee," "Kimono/Chong Sum," "Kabuki/Chinese Opera," and "Short Grain Rice/Long Grain Rice."

The sixth and final comparison is Marlon Brando playing the Japanese character Sakini in the movie *The Teahouse of the August Moon*. A voice with a Japanese accent states, "This is Marlon Brando." The voice with a Chinese accent then states, "Marlon Brando is not Chinese." The voice with the Japanese accent states, "Marlon Brando is not Japanese either!" A picture slide stating, "NOT JAPANESE," appears on the video monitor and changes to a yellow picture slide. Then the TV monitor depicts American actor Sidney Toler playing the role of Charlie Chan, who was featured in twenty-two films after the Swedish actor popularized the character beginning in 1931. A voice with a Chinese accents states, "This is Sidney Toler." A voice with a Japanese accent states, "Sidney Toler is not Japanese," and the voice with a Chinese accent states, "Sidney Toler is not Chinese either!" A picture slide stating, "NOT CHINESE" appears, and the TV monitor goes to yellow. The voice with the Chinese accent ends the performance by saying, "Shei shei" and then "Thank you," and the voice with the Japanese accent says, "Arigato gozaimasu" and then "Thank you." Both slide images and screen go to black.

Shimomura highlights the cultural advantages white male actors have in U.S. popular culture, as neither Japanese nor Chinese characters are played by Asian American actors. More troubling is the lack of visual presence of Asian Americans in U.S. popular culture as well as their history. Shimomura further illuminates the lack of cultural acceptance for Asian American culture by pointing to this inherent discrimination. "Yellow No (All) Same" directly analyzes racism in the United States, where Asians and Asian Americans are stereotyped, generalized, and considered the same. By pointing out basic differences such as language, flag, national leaders, food, attire, and popular entertainers, Shimomura is not merely pointing to cultural differences among different Asian groups, but he is also addressing the larger systemic issues of racial and discriminatory attitudes that affect the sociocultural and political lives of Asian Americans.

The closing video and conclusion of "Make Rice, Not War" begins with the video monitor fading in to a close-up of an Asian girl carrying an electric rice cooker, hammer, model airplane, and Mickey Mouse doll and running down a country road, while the first verse of Fats Waller's "Ain't Misbehavin'" (1929) is heard instrumentally [IMAGE 77]. Opposite the opening video, the girl gradually retreats from the camera over a five-minute period. As the second verse of "Ain't Misbehavin'" is heard with Fats Waller singing, a spotlit kurogo walks to the rice cooker and quickly places a bowl, cups, napkins, and spoon on the table before efficiently serving the rice-and-toy-soldier concoction into the bowl, removing the rice cooker and leaving the bowl, cups, and napkins before exiting the theater. The video continues for another thirty seconds, and the bowl of rice and toy soldiers remains illuminated by the spotlight until the video ends [IMAGE 78].

Shimomura reverses the audience's opening connection to the Asian girl as she now moves away from the camera. Furthermore, the musical selection has changed from a symbol of the model minority myth, the astronomically successful Yo-Yo Ma, to the more comical and rebellious nature of Fats Waller's upbeat, jazzy, love song, "Ain't Misbehavin'." Shimomura creates tension between what is seen and heard, as Waller's "Ain't Misbehavin'" is intended to maintain his relationship with his lover, although the sincerity of Waller's lyrics and title makes the intent questionable. Shimomura depicts the girl holding these highly symbolic objects while retreating from the audience, and her future actions are equally questionable and unknown. Shimomura gives the power of ownership to the Asian girl as she holds these objects, and what she is to do with them is left to her discretion.

On the other hand, Shimomura examines the actions of the U.S. government and popular culture by analyzing American foundational values of the

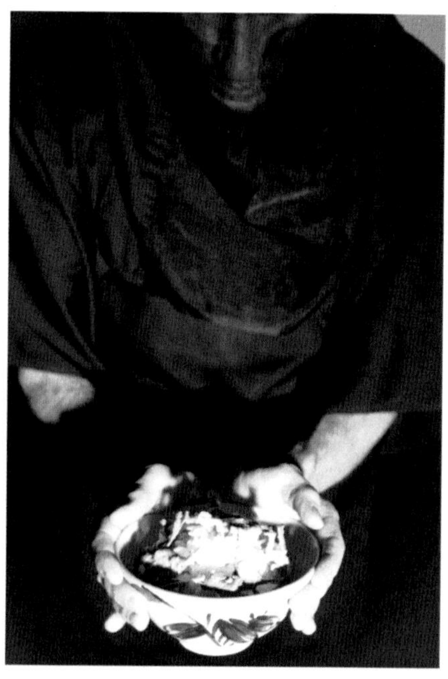

Above, IMAGE 77: Detail; right, IMAGE 78: Detail.

(Photographs by Roger Shimomura, *California Sushi*, photographs, January 10-13, 1990, Franklin Furnace: New York City, New York).

freedom, liberty, and equality of all of its citizens. A continuation of the initial act, “Make Rice, Not War” is a final reminder and further symbolism of the horrors of World War II on the Japanese American experience, their (Asian American) entanglement with nationalistic policy and militarism, and the artist’s darkly humorous reference to the human value of making peace over war. Comparing the racist portrayal of Asian Americans within U.S. material culture, Waller’s song’s lyrics, “Ain’t Misbehavin’,” may be applied to the behavior and sincerity of the U.S. government as questionable, especially as it pertains to perceiving young Asian American citizens with their love of Disney and toys as dangerous. This tension is precisely what Shimomura sets out to examine in this body of short performances.

Through *California Sushi*, Shimomura is able to preserve histories and memories often unknown by non-Asian Americans. Although critical of some perceptions of cultural mixing, the artist is not nostalgic for tradition. Instead, Shimomura is a bellwether for one point of view that reminds Americans of their racial past—not as a scarlet letter, but rather in the hope that such actions can be learned from and not repeated. Shimomura created *California Sushi* to address his past in a constructive manner, not to perpetuate racial stereotyping or differences, but through the utilization of popular culture, parody, and dark humor to highlight the absurdity of racial attitudes in hopes that viewers walk away with a greater level of cultural sensitivity to difference.

Tony Allard as Hawaiian (Photograph by Roger Shimomura, *Campfire Diary*, April 7-8, 1994, Main Auditorium, Walker Art Center: Minneapolis, Minnesota).

6

campfire diary

- River Room, Wichita Art Museum, Wichita, Kansas, November 21, 1992
- Cheney Cowles Museum, Spokane, Washington, February 18, 1993
- Dr. Lester S. Baskin Hall, Tacoma Art Museum, Tacoma, Washington, February 23, 1993
- Bertha Martin Theater, University of Northern Iowa, Cedar Falls, Iowa, September 11, 1993
- The Theater, Johnson Community College, Overland Park, Kansas, October 15, 1993
- Main Auditorium, Walker Art Center, Minneapolis, Minnesota, April 7–8, 1994
- Carmichael Auditorium, Smithsonian Institution, National Museum of American History, Washington, DC, February 24, 1995
- Space for Dance, Colorado Dance Festival, Boulder, Colorado, March 15–16, 1995
- Taos Community Auditorium, Taos Art Association, Taos, New Mexico, March 21, 1995
- Center for Contemporary Art, Santa Fe, New Mexico, March 23–24, 1995
- Directed and presented by Joel Sanderson, Wichita Center for the Arts, Wichita, Kansas, June 21–22, 1996

Campfire Diary, 1992, is a rewrite of Shimomura's *Seven Kabuki Plays Project* and the "Moon Seen as Exiles" act from *Tran-Siberian Excerpts.* Revisiting his early work, Shimomura is able to create a more dynamic, succinct, and emotive performance about his grandmother Toku Shimomura's experience of the Japanese American incarceration. He uses the same six diary entries from Toku's journal, spanning Japan's attack on Pearl Harbor to her first Christmas spent as an incarcerated prisoner of the United States with no just cause. Shimomura utilizes his trademark iconography,

hybrid audio compositions, and costume designs, as well as the entire theater, to offer a panoramic experience that engulfs his audience.

Part One

Part One opens with the audience finding their seats among Roy Lichtenstein's projected paintings depicting World War II American fighter planes that cover the ceiling, along with haunting music that evokes the pending combat that is about to ensue. In *Campfire Diary*, Shimomura blends the iconic pop art that is associated more closely with U.S. comics and branding than the horrors of actual warfare experienced by Japanese American citizens to invite the audience into the historical recoding offered by his performance art. Once the audience is seated, the music fades away as Kurogo 1 turns off the slide projectors one at a time until the room is dark.

In the darkness, the first diary entry is read in Japanese in its entirety and followed by the sounds of aircraft approaching. Presumably the audience cannot understand Japanese, and Shimomura signals their distance from this history as well as Toku's perspective.

On the large screen, a video montage begins, depicting historical footage of Japanese airplanes headed toward Pearl Harbor. This historical footage alternates with popular-culture video footage, such as the actress Jane Seymour wearing a kimono and bowing, and then back again to footage of the attack and bombings at Pearl Harbor, then alternating again to mundane footage of Japanese rockabillies dancing in the streets of Japan to rock and roll music and wearing U.S. greaser-style clothes and hairstyles [IMAGES 80-83].

During the video montage, the first diary entry is read again, but this time in English: "December 7, 1941: When I came home from church, I heard the dreamlike news that Japanese airplanes had bombed Pearl Harbor. I was surprised beyond belief. I sat in front of the radio and listened to the news all day. It was said that at 6:00 a.m. Japan declared war on the United States." Shimomura's stark contrast of the banal ways the United States and Japan influence each other's culture, with the catalyst of these cultural intersections, and specifically the horrific tragedy of the attack on Pearl Harbor, is meant to not only operate as a recreation of Toku's life at that time, which

Top left, IMAGE 80: Video of the Bombing of Pearl Harbor, December 7, 1941; top right, IMAGE 81: Video of Jayne Seymour; bottom left, IMAGE 82: Video of the Bombing of Pearl Harbor, December 7, 1941; bottom right, IMAGE 83: Video of Japanese rockabillies.

(All photographs by Roger Shimomura, *Campfire Diary*, April 7-8, 1994, Main Auditorium, Walker Art Center: Minneapolis, Minnesota).

has been suddenly and forever changed, but also to allude to the absence of the Japanese American experience, which Toku's journals occupy, from mainstream history. Instead, Shimomura points to unusual cultural intersections and a historical void that fails to portray Japanese Americans.

As the historic video footage of the Pearl Harbor attack continues to alternate with scenes from *Madame Butterfly* (with a Caucasian-only cast playing the role of Japanese characters), and then back to Pearl Harbor scenes before shifting to a *My Three Sons* episode showing a Caucasian boy dancing with a Japanese girl. Kurogo 2 shines a spotlight onto a man with binoculars wearing a straw hat, lei, and aloha shirt, who watches the screen for thirty seconds before the spotlight goes out. As the video montage continues to alternate back and forth between scenes of Caucasians learning to dance Japanese Kabuki and women's professional wrestling in Japan, Kurogo 2 then turns the spotlight back on the man, who is now wearing a white mask as well and holding a microphone [IMAGE 84]. He begins to lip sync Don Ho's "Tiny Bubbles" as the audio track is played. The video continues to shift

Top, IMAGE 84: Tony Allard as Don Ho.

Bottom, IMAGE 85: Tony Allard as Hawaiian.

(Photographs by Roger Shimomura, *Campfire Diary*, April 7-8, 1994, Main Auditorium, Walker Art Center: Minneapolis, Minnesota).

back and forth between Pearl Harbor and a cowboy, Indian, and samurai fight scene—and then Sesame Street's Big Bird visiting Japan—until the lip sync of the song is over, and the video fades to black. Shimomura showcases the breadth of cultural interactions between Japan and the United States in popular culture, and what seems banal and frivolous quickly reveals subtle power hierarchies and cultural tensions. Shimomura adds these symbolic layers of meaning to evoke both the banal and horrific aspects of Toku's life as a Japanese American that suddenly and unexpectedly collided through war, shattering her world.

Shimomura recodes the structure of theater by reversing the passive experience of the audience watching a performance, turning the audience into the subject being watched. As *Campfire Diary* continues, the video projection fades in from black and portrays the aloha-shirt performer, now peering through his binoculars out at the audience, surveying them as they become the object of scrutiny [IMAGE 85]. Shimomura carefully shifts the power of the Gaze, from the audience/viewer to the performer/actor. Toku's diary entry in English continues, "Our future has become gloomy. I pray God will stay with us." Toku uses the pronoun 'our' to include the audience in the story, as they are now part of the performance. Before the theater fades to complete darkness, off in the distance, Roosevelt's broadcast is heard: "Yesterday, December 7th, a date which will live in infamy..." and the room is silent and dark. The role reversal, coupled with Toku's diary entry, allows the audience to take Toku's position as the watched Japanese American, whose loyalty is questioned, civil rights are taken, and life is forever changed. Shimomura, evoking the historic and life-changing event of Pearl Harbor, moves the audience from a passive to an active participant in his performance art. Shimomura recodes and reverses meaning to dismantle power structures that are often overlooked and unquestioned: audience/performer, history/fiction, Japanese/American, banal/meaningful, popular culture/art, entertainment/real-life tragedy. He uses these strategies to create new meaning, for example, from what is common and assumed (the attack on Pearl Harbor), to what is unknown and unseen (the Japanese American experience).

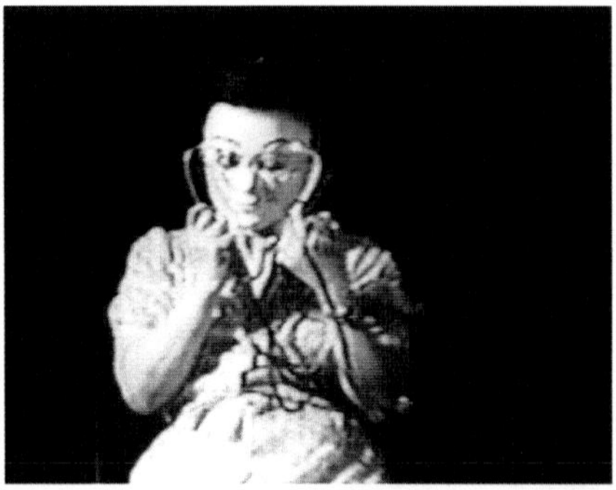

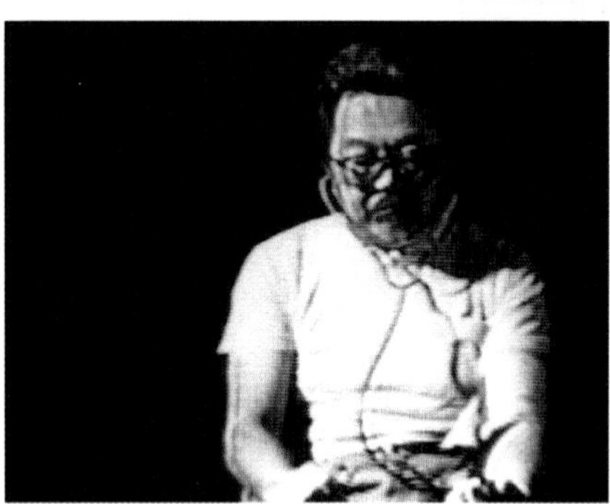

Top, IMAGE 86: Tony Allard as Toku.

Center, IMAGE 87: Tony Allard as Superman.

Bottom, IMAGE 88: Roger Shimomura, age 50.

(All photographs by Roger Shimomura, *Campfire Diary*, April 7-8, 1994, Main Auditorium, Walker Art Center: Minneapolis, Minnesota).

Part Two

Part Two begins with the reciting of Toku's second diary entry in Japanese, accompanied by the sound of a heartbeat and followed by ominous music. Projected on the screen is video of Toku checking her blood pressure as a voice states, "My blood pressure was 190 over 110 [IMAGE 86]." Toku bows her head in disappointment and sighs before the video fades to black. In English, the second diary entry is partially read: "December 12, 1941: I spent all day at home. Starting from today we were permitted to withdraw one hundred dollars from the bank. I deeply felt America's large-heartedness in dealing with us." Then, patriotic music and drumming begin, while an image of a shoji and the silhouette of Superman flexing his muscles appears [IMAGE 87]. Kurogo 1 flies an inflated life-sized doll of Superman through the audience, throwing money in his wake while spotlit by Kurogo 2. Shimomura uses parody and dark humor to interpret Toku's words, as the U.S. government (Superman) is neither heroic nor generous in its treatment of Japanese Americans by permitting them access to their personally earned money. Kurogo 1 and 2 exit with Superman, and the video fades to black as the sound of a heartbeat is again heard. A video projection of Roger Shimomura taking his blood pressure appears on the screen. Roger says, "My blood pressure was 210 over 120," and, paralleling Toku, he bows his head and sighs in defeat [IMAGE 88]. Shimomura contrasts this depressing scene with patriotic music and heightened-tempo drumming before ending the piece in silence. Shimomura draws a connection between his grandmother's hypertension and his own more highly elevated hypertension to demonstrate not only their familial connection and his memories of her, but also the lasting effects of the U.S. government's actions toward Japanese Americans. As a nurse, Toku monitored and recorded her health as part of her daily journal entries, making her diary unusual in the medical perspective and documentation they afford of her fifty-nine years as an immigrant in the United States. Shimomura makes this central to the act to personalize *Campfire Diary* and to medically and physically convey the unprecedented trauma of World War II in Toku's life and the lives of all persons affected by war.

Part Three

Part Three opens with Toku's diary entry recited in Japanese as the sound of drumming and flashes of a picture slide of a shoji are projected on the screen to the beat of the drum. In English, the audio voice reads the third diary entry: "February 3, 1942: I finally decided to do my fingerprint registration since it had been hanging heavily on my mind. I went to the post office with Mrs. Sakai." The shoji is projected again as the background, and in the foreground a woman performer dressed in 1940s clothing stands frozen. A video silhouette of a woman dressed in traditional kimono and coiffure initially follows her like a shadow as she moves across the stage, eventually preceding her identity as a U.S. immigrant [IMAGE 89]. Shimomura again uses the notion of "the power of Gaze" to portray how the U.S. government viewed Toku, as a traditional Japanese woman, versus the way Toku presented herself as a member of U.S. society as she literally steps out of the projection of a traditional Japanese woman, and yet is unable to escape the shadow or gaze as Other.[59]

As the scene changes, fading in from black, the projection of a fingerprint against a yellow background appears, overlaid by a second fingerprint that moves in a seemingly psychedelic, circular pattern. The audience hears the rest of the diary entry in English: "We finished the strict registration at 11:00 a.m. I feel that a heavy load has been taken off my mind." Toku stands in the center of the projection and walks out toward the audience, like a zombie character, with her hands held out, exposing all ten fingers covered with black ink, and eventually exiting through the back of the theater [IMAGE 90]. Shimomura symbolizes the psychedelic horror that Toku experienced in having to register her identity for a second time with the U.S. government; however, now she is viewed as a monstrous threat to the U.S. society that Shimomura carefully parodies.

Part Four

In Part Four, Toku's diary entry is recited in Japanese, and a picture slide of barbed wire is projected on the screen. Slow and sad music is heard among distant sounds of thunder. Flashes of the flagpole at Minidoka, Idaho, during the daily flag-lowering ceremony are seen [IMAGE 91]. With each flash the camera moves in closer until the "retreat" song played on the bugle and the sounds of the storm increase in their intensity before the theater fades to black. Shimomura cues the audience to the new location of the Shimomura family at the Minidoka incarceration center and evokes the sadness and metaphoric storm that they are encountering.

As the depressing music continues, the video projection changes to an interior wall of the barracks with a window. The standard look of the wall

Top, IMAGE 89: Tony Allard as Toku.

Center, IMAGE 90: Tony Allard as Toku.

Bottom, IMAGE 91: Video of Flag Salute, Minidoka, Idaho.

(All photographs by Roger Shimomura, *Campfire Diary*, April 7-8, 1994, Main Auditorium, Walker Art Center: Minneapolis, Minnesota).

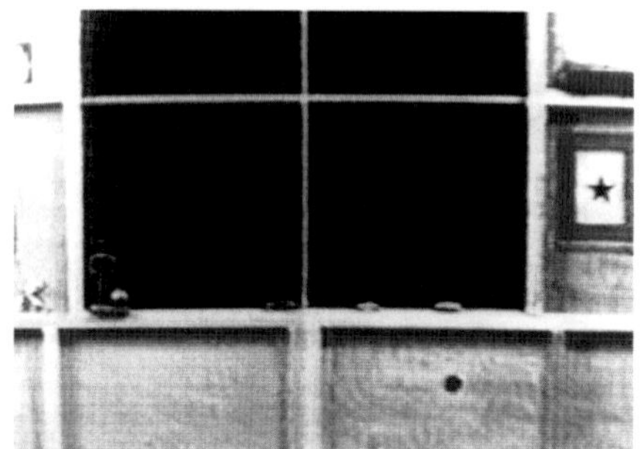

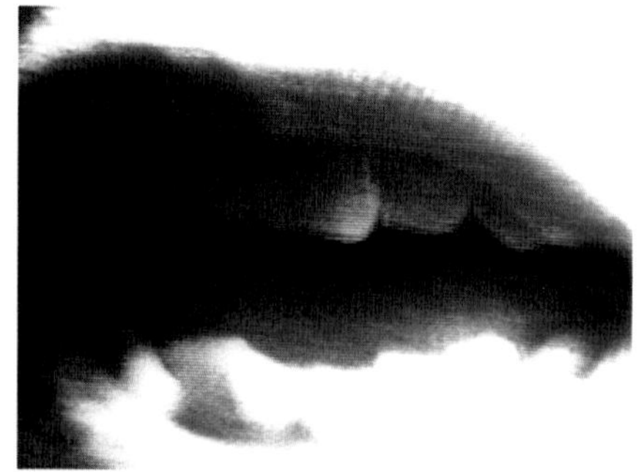

Top left and right, IMAGES 92 and 93: Details.

Center, IMAGE 94: Detail.

Bottom, IMAGE 95: Tony Allard as Issei.

(All photographs by Roger Shimomura, *Campfire Diary*, April 7-8, 1994, Main Auditorium, Walker Art Center: Minneapolis, Minnesota).

consisted of exposed wood framing and sheer wall, covered in black tarpaper [IMAGES 92-93]. Internees decorated their living quarters, as shown here, with personal items such as photos, a couple of small toy cars (in this particular case, referencing Roger as a toddler), and a U.S. military veteran star (Roger's father). As the music changes to a slow, lyrical flute melody and grinding cacophonous sounds, the camera zooms in and out on these objects. Shimomura uses these dichotomous sounds to signal that something is wrong with this picture. In English, the audio voice reads the partial diary entry: "August 27, 1942: Storm, what a view. I have never seen such a dust storm." The seemingly tranquil interior shows nothing of the harsh environment beyond the thin, sheer wall.

As the projection fades to black, Toku the performer steps in front of the screen, aligning herself perfectly with the now-illuminated image of Toku in the projection of the same barracks room. The diary entry continues, "I stayed in my room and looked out of the window," while Toku the performer begins to walk off-stage, as if coming to life from the projection, the projected image of Toku is left behind to look out the window [IMAGE 94]. Shimomura uses the transformative power of performance art to play with the narrative; he gives Toku the ability to walk off-stage and out of the harsh environment, as a metaphor for us all having the power to learn from the past and create a better future. In Shimomura's *Campfire Diary*, Toku is liberated from her past.

Shimomura continues to use the power of performance art to blur the boundary between art and life. Toku's diary entry states, "It was so dark we were all afraid to move." The theater goes dark, and Shimomura takes away the comfort of electricity and sight, and the audience once again becomes part of the performance—part of Toku's experience. The reading continues, "Pessimistic words came out of everyone's mouth." The audio plays a dramatic chord, and the video projection shows a close-up of a woman's mouth [IMAGE 95]. In Japanese, the audio and mouth say simultaneously, "We were sent to such a harsh place!" The audio plays a dramatic chord again, and the video goes black. Then the close-up of the mouth along with the Japanese voice repeats the same phrase two more times in a row. On the fourth recitation, "We were sent to such a harsh place!" is said in English so the audience can understand Toku's diary entry. This is immediately followed by sounds of thunder, dramatic musical chords and, then silence. Shimomura recreates the Japanese American experience through a

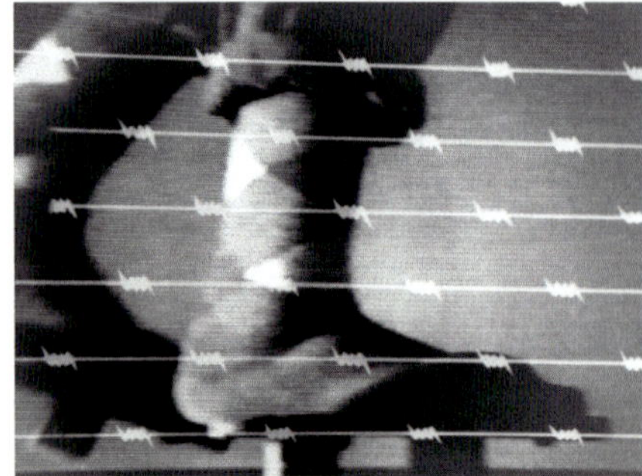

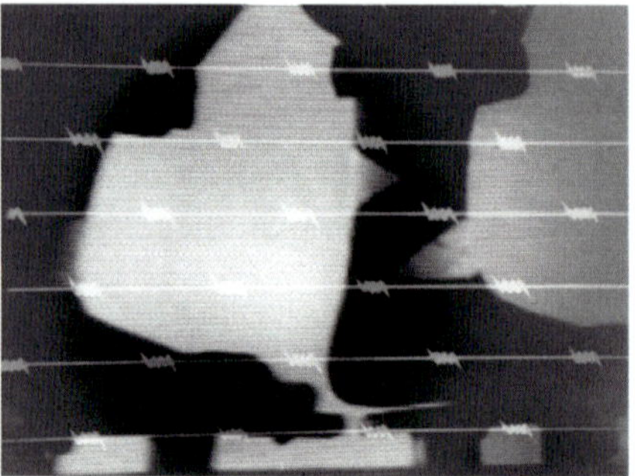

Top left and right, IMAGES 96-97: Tony Allard as Issei.

Bottom, IMAGE 98: Tony Allard as Kabuki actor.

(All photographs by Roger Shimomura, *Campfire Diary*, April 7-8, 1994, Main Auditorium, Walker Art Center: Minneapolis, Minnesota).

dynamic reimagining of the rules of theater: images come to life, audience becomes the performance, and history is reborn.

Part Five

Part Five similarly begins with Toku's diary entry read in Japanese while an image of barbed wire is projected onto the screen, symbolizing the incarceration center. The video shows feet wearing argyle socks and walking in geta (Japanese shoes) against a blue background [IMAGES 96-97]. In

English, the audio voice reads Toku's entry: "May 23, 1942: It was clear today. As always the day was monotonous. During the evening Ogishima and I paid a visit to Kuboto-san who was ill." Video fades to black and then back to the same feet walking against a gray background. Continuing, the audio voice reads Toku's diary entry, "Even if you are not healthy, it is not very pleasant nowadays." As sounds of rain start, Kurogo 2 illuminates a Kabuki actor holding an umbrella [IMAGE 98]. They walk across the stage and then down the aisle, exiting the back of the theater. Reading more of Toku's entry, "I went to bed listening to the sounds of raindrops, which sounded like machine guns." The sounds of rain morph into machine gun fire and then fade along with the projection to black. Shimomura focuses on the juxtaposition of U.S. and Japanese culture through the combination of argyle socks and geta as symbolic of the Japanese American experience. He uses the background colors to signify day and night as well as the rapidly decaying attitudes of internees. The metaphoric irony comes from the banal sounds of rain that Toku likens to machine guns. The incarceration centers were in the most remote and desolate habitats, and as Toku described in Part Four, were harsh places with minimal resources, removed from the arenas of war. However, there were guard towers with guns pointed inward at the internees to keep them imprisoned, not to protect them from external threats. The irony was that the Japanese Americans were imprisoned and treated as enemies, and yet they would soon thereafter be employed by the U.S. government to fight for American liberty and democracy, which was ripped away from their lives.

Part Six

Part Six also opens with the Japanese recitation of Toku's journal entry and the slide projection of barbed wire, still indicating her imprisonment at Minidoka. The Christmas lights adorning the perimeter of the screen are turned on, and tense music starts. In English, the first part of Toku's entry is read: "December 25, 1942: The muddy ground was completely covered by the white snow. It was like a beautiful white cloth and a suitable sight for Christmas." A scene from the 1940s film *The Night Before Christmas*, playing in reverse, is projected on top of the barbed-wire picture slide, symbolizing the backwardness of this event. The next part of Toku's entry is read: "We sat happily at the family table," while the left screen portrays a shoji and a silhouetted image of a family sitting to eat dinner as the tense music continues [IMAGE 99]. Shimomura symbolizes the perception of Japanese Americans celebrating Christmas at Minidoka through the lens of

IMAGE 99: Tony Allard as Santa Claus (Photograph by Roger Shimomura, *Campfire Diary*, April 7-8, 1994, Main Auditorium, Walker Art Center: Minneapolis, Minnesota).

a shoji, symbolic of their Japaneseness. After the film clip ends, the barbed wire remains and Toku's diary entry continues, "At 9:00 p.m. Santa Claus appeared. For these few moments I forgot where I was." Shimomura contrasts the tense music with Toku's few moments of bliss that permitted her to forget the reality of her incarceration. Shimomura contrasts the meaning of Christmas—not as the commercialized event but rather bringing happiness to others and not thinking of oneself—in honor of the nativity of Christ, a man destined to sacrifice himself for all of humanity, and the context of the situation as incarcerated Japanese Americans. Toku was a devout Christian and mentions God often in her diary entries. The incarcerated Japanese Americans collectively made this Christmas for one another to enjoy, which brought so much happiness to them that Toku momentarily forgot the horror of her reality.

The music shifts to "Silent Night," played on a flute as Santa Claus emerges between the two shoji, handing out origami cranes folded out of Mickey Mouse wrapping paper. Shimomura blends the notion of Santa Claus with the Japanese symbolism of a thousand origami cranes to grant a wish—both symbols that bring happiness to others. The artist also combines the art of origami with an American popular-culture icon, Disney, to signify the awkward cultural combinations of the Japanese American experiences, especially that of a toddler, as Shimomura was three years old.

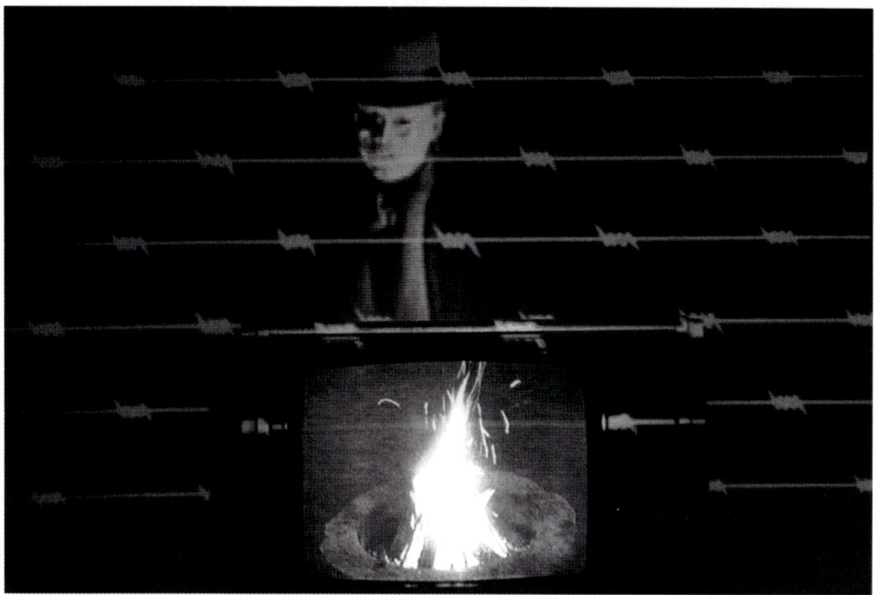

IMAGE 100: Tony Allard as Old Man (Photograph by Roger Shimomura, *Campfire Diary*, April 7-8, 1994, Main Auditorium, Walker Art Center: Minneapolis, Minnesota).

Part Seven

Part Seven opens with slow, melancholy music and Kurogo 2 pushing a TV monitor in front of the screen. Once in position, the television is turned on and depicts a campfire, while the projection of barbed wire appears on the screen for the final time. A video of a man wearing a mask and dressed in an overcoat and hat appears from the darkness in front of the barbed wire [IMAGE 100]. In Japanese, the poem "Moon Seen as Exiles" is read. It was written in Japanese by an anonymous internee and documented in Toku's journals. After the recitation is complete, Kurogo 2 turns off the campfire on the television, and the projection fades to black. Shimomura keeps the man's identity anonymous and presents the poem in Japanese, as it was originally composed.

Then the side stage is illuminated, depicting a faux campfire and a boy doll, dressed in Western clothes and operated by Kurogo 1 [IMAGE 101]. In English, a male voice recites the poem, while the doll moves his head and arms, listening along.

> *Here in Minidoka in Idaho,*
> *on the high plains with sagebrush,*
> *packs of coyotes roam at night.*

IMAGE 101: Tony Allard as Kurogo (Photograph by Roger Shimomura, *Campfire Diary*, April 7-8, 1994, Main Auditorium, Walker Art Center: Minneapolis, Minnesota).

Even though spring comes, no flowers bloom.
In summer, strong winds whirl;
in winter, snowstorms hit our windows.

Bearing on our backs the word enemy,
we ten thousand, wire-fenced in,
endure a wretched life severed from yesteryear.

In fifty years of endeavor and work,
we had built a foundation.
Abandoning it, we watch the moon. Exiles.

No matter how hard our pains,
we sacrifice under national policy,
taking each other's hands, vowing to endure.

When the breeze of peace blows,
spring with blooming flowers will come around.
Then our pains will become a tale of past dreams.[60]

When the recitation is over, the spotlight goes to black, and the campfire is extinguished. Audio of drums and a bugle begin. In Japanese, the following words are recited: *samui* ("cold"), *atsui* ("hot"), *hokori darake* ("dusty"), *kaze-ga tsuyoi* ("windy"), *sabishii* ("lonely"), *hito ga ippai* ("crowded"), and *shikata ga nai* ("it is beyond our control"). The final sound of airplanes passing overhead ends *Campfire Dairy*, as if to signal the last line of the poem, "Then our pains will become a tale of past dreams." This wish of the anonymous internee is an unanswerable question that Shimomura leaves open to interpretation: Will their pains become a tale of past dreams?

The poem concludes *Campfire Diary* as another layer of primary evidence corroborating Toku's dairy entries documenting the experience of Japanese Americans during incarceration. Shimomura chose the term "campfire" to recall the telling of stories, specifically oral history, around a campfire, and in this way Shimomura passes on his family's history. Shimomura also uses "campfire" to refer to the euphemism "camp" that was used by the U.S. government to describe the ten incarceration centers where over one hundred twenty thousand Japanese Americans were imprisoned. He parodies the absurdity of drawing parallels between the leisurely act of camping and the horrific conditions of being imprisoned, named an "enemy" of the state, and losing your livelihood without any just cause. Shimomura gives the last words of the piece to Japanese Americans, using Japanese words to describe their incarceration experience.

Shimomura collaborated with Joel Sanderson, composer; Tony Allard, solo performer; and Ione Unruh, costume designer. Funding was made possible by the National Endowment for the Arts, the Rockefeller Foundation, the Andy Warhol Foundation, DiverseWorks, Art Matters Inc. Grant, the University of Kansas, General Research Fund; the University of Kansas, Faculty Scholarship Travel Fund; and the University of Kansas, School of Fine Arts.

Family Photograph of Roger and Toku
(*The Last Sansei Story*, April 20, 1993, Haskell
Indian Junior College: Lawrence, Kansas).

7 the last sansei story

- **Haskell Indian Junior College, sponsored by the University of Kansas New Directions Series, Lawrence, Kansas, April 20, 1993**
- **The Theater, Johnson Community College, Overland Park, Kansas, October 16, 1993**

Shimomura's *The Last Sansei Story* is the largest multimedia performance art piece created by the artist to date, and similarly, it addresses an expansive topic of the sociohistorical aspects of the Japanese American experience. *The Last Sansei Story* is broken into three acts paralleling the three generations (Issei, Nisei, and Sansei) of Japanese Americans. Shimomura calls the performance, *The Last Sansei Story* because there will neither be the economic conditions sparking the enormous immigration of Japanese workers to the United States, nor will three generations of any group of people experience such traumatic and life-changing events, bookmarked between two world wars.[61]

The Last Sansei Story incorporates Shimomura's vast personal collection of popular-culture materials—such as video, film, picture slides, writing, audio tapes, and kitsch discussing cross-cultural topics—and his family's (even more vast) oral and written history that includes his grandmother Toku (Machida) Shimomura's fifty-six years of daily diary entries, Toku's published and unpublished written stories, family photographs, and audiotapes of Toku and her husband, Yoshitomi Shimomura. The artist's intention for *The Last Sansei Story* is to foster dialogue around topics pertaining to the Japanese American experience using the transformative power of performance art.[62] One technique Shimomura employs throughout the performance is making the audience active participants in the performance. The artist includes the audience to initiate the dissemination of information, create moments of transference of meaning between the performance and reality, and ultimately, effect new perceptions.

Prelude: Grandma's Story, Port Arthur, 1904

The Last Sansei Story begins with a prelude to introduce Shimomura's grandmother, an Issei woman immigrant, and the main impetus not only for the artist's existence (as Toku came out of retirement as a midwife to deliver Roger) but also a significant portion of his vast body of work. Compared to other historical narratives of the Japanese American experience in the 1990s, it was rare to have an Issei, female perspective covering the experience of "picture brides."[63] In the prelude, Shimomura provides historical and personal insight into Toku's character—as a volunteer Red Cross nurse, articulating her charitable devotion to people in need, as well as her bravery and valor as a volunteer on the front lines of the Russo-Japanese War.

The prelude begins with the curtain going up and a yellow spotlight appearing on a shoji. Kurogo 1 and 2 open the biparting screens and then exit. To the left of the stage, a title slide appears, that reads, "Prelude: Grandma's Story, Port Arthur, 1904" [IMAGE 103]. Shimomura uses Russo-Japanese War-themed music and projects Russia's and Japan's flags side-by-side as a historical marker [IMAGE 104]. A performer depicting Toku Shimomura appears on stage dressed as a Red Cross nurse, along with Kurogos 1, 2, and 3, as the music shifts to reflect the nursing profession [IMAGE 105]. Toku's voice states, "I was a member of the twenty-fifth graduating class of the Red Cross Nursing School. The Russo-Japanese War began before my graduation." Toku mimes the story on stage and above her is a large, projected photograph of Toku and her graduating class, as the kurogos simulate a rolling wave across the entire stage with a piece of blue fabric [IMAGE 106]. This was a significant battle, as it was the first time an Asian navy defeated a European navy.

IMAGE 103: Detail (Photograph by Roger Shimomura, *The Last Sansei Story*, April 20, 1993, Haskell Indian Junior College: Lawrence, Kansas).

Top, IMAGE 104: Detail.

Center, IMAGE 105: Photograph of Toku and Graduating Class as a Nurse for the Red Cross.

Bottom, IMAGE 106: Marsha Paludan as Toku.

(All photographs by Roger Shimomura, *The Last Sansei Story,* April 20, 1993, Haskell Indian Junior College: Lawrence, Kansas).

Top, IMAGE 107: Detail.

Center, IMAGE 108: Marsha Paludan as Toku.

Bottom, IMAGE 109: Detail.

(All photographs by Roger Shimomura, *The Last Sansei Story*, April 20, 1993, Haskell Indian Junior College: Lawrence, Kansas).

IMAGE 110: Detail (Photographs by Roger Shimomura, *The Last Sansei Story*, April 20, 1993, Haskell Indian Junior College: Lawrence, Kansas).

Toku continues to mime her story alongside her oral history, revealing her service and bravery to the Japanese Navy. She was drafted as a member of the twenty-first relief squad and boarded the *Yokohama Maru*. Japan's naval fleet set out to challenge the Russian Navy before they reached the Japanese archipelago. On their journey up the Tsushima Channel, the *Yokohama Maru* encountered the Baltic fleet and docked on the Hagi shore of the Yamaguchi Prefecture as the battle unfolded before their eyes. To simulate watching the battle through a telescope, Shimomura projects circular-shaped picture slides of sea battle paintings that fade in and out while cannon fire plays [IMAGE 107]. Throughout the night, and in the early morning, the nursing team waits for news. Japan's victory brings tears to the entire nursing team, but the traumas and devastation of war abound in Toku's mind. The end of her monologue states, "The Sea of Genkai was rolling with large waves quite as usual, but we saw fragments of broken masts of the enemy fleet, and possessions of Russian soldiers, floating in the water. Unconsciously we folded our hands in awe and prayer as we passed the place where the fierce battle had raged" [IMAGE 108]. Toku's words are significant primary resources and help the audience feel the pathos of war. During this terrifying period of time, Japan and Toku's Red Cross team were on the "winning" side of the war, although her monologue demonstrates that war is less about victory and more about the person-to-person toll on humanity. Contrasting Toku's two wartime experiences as a Japanese citizen and nurse in the Russo-Japanese War during the beginning of her life, with her unjust incarceration as an "enemy alien" in World War II at the end of her career, shows these two extreme and pivotal moments in her life.

Part One: "The Issei"

Part One: "The Issei" begins with side-by-side video and slide projections accompanied by music and a live performer [IMAGES 109-10]. Shimomura creates a multimedia, multisensory, and, multilayered iconographic introduction to the act. The video projection portrays a juggler dressed in a

IMAGE 111: Detail (Photograph by Roger Shimomura, *The Last Sansei Story,* April 20, 1993, Haskell Indian Junior College: Lawrence, Kansas).

kimono and wearing an Asian face mask while juggling three objects, accompanied by circus music [IMAGE 111]. He juggles a baseball, *kokeshi* doll (Japanese wooden doll), and a *daruma* (Japanese good-luck charm). On the left side of the stage are a projected title slide that reads, "The Issei," and a picture slide of the three objects being juggled. The objects are symbolic of the first generation, Issei, who Shimomura suggests are one-third American and two-thirds Japanese. The notion of the "Americanness" of Japanese Americans and how this changes with each generation is a central topic of Shimomura's *The Last Sansei Story.*

As the music fades, along with the slide and video projections, a Euro-American version of traditional Japanese theater music begins, and a spotlight illuminates a performer dressed in a Noh (traditional Japanese theater) mask, Heian-style kimono, and modern-day headphones, as he begins his walk down the aisle from the back of the theater toward the stage [IMAGE 112]. With a multilayered approach, Shimomura uses music, costume, and elements of Japanese theater to signal the cultural mixing between Japanese and U.S. culture, past and present, as symbolic of the Issei immigrant experience.

The Noh dancer freezes after approximately fifteen seconds, the room fades to black, and the music goes silent. A ship's horn sounds and slow music begins as a picture slide introduces another aspect of the Issei experience, "Immigration: The Picture Brides." The audio voice reads Toku's diary entry in English:

> *February 28, 1912: The wind and rain fell angrily. The visitors came continuously from early morning. Sister Tachi from Tokyo and Sister Honma from Kanagawa came all the way to see me off. I said farewell to both of them and embarked. The rain splattered down. The skies were partly clear. Only the wind was severe. As the ship departed, we wished each other health by waving handkerchiefs until we could*

Top, IMAGE 112: Kentaro Fukada as Noh Actor; left, IMAGE 113: Marsha Paludan as Toku; right, IMAGE 114: Issei Picture Brides.

(All photographs by Roger Shimomura, *The Last Sansei Story*, April 20, 1993, Haskell Indian Junior College: Lawrence, Kansas).

> *no longer see one another. I hurried back to my room as I could not bear the heartbreaking pain. I felt a little seasick. After prayers of thanks, I went to bed.*[64]

Toku wears a Noh mask, Mickey Mouse ears, a kimono, and a large white cross around her neck symbolizing her proximity to Japanese culture and Christianity, a Western religion [IMAGE 113]. During the recitation of the journal entry, she dances in front of a shoji screen. Notably, the cross-cultural interaction between Japan and the United States is already present in Toku's life.[65] Another topic Shimomura presents is Japan's familiarity with Western culture through mechanisms like Christianity prior to immigration.

As the scene changes to the immigration dance, Toku exits, and dramatic drums and crashing symbols accompany picture-slide projections of close-up details of Katsushika Hokusai's "The Great Wave off Kanagawa" from his "Thirty-Six Views of Mount Fuji" series [IMAGE 114]. Overhead, six

IMAGE 115: Kari Paludan as Cinderella (Photograph by Roger Shimomura, *The Last Sansei Story*, April 20, 1993, Haskell Indian Junior College: Lawrence, Kansas).

photographs showing six husbands are illuminated. Five female picture brides enter the theater from the rear and sides and throw streamers at the audience before making their way to the stage, where they will be joined by Toku to perform the the picture bride dance. Their costumes are composed of an odd amalgamation of Japanese and American cultural references: yellow kimonos, Mickey Mouse ears, yellow backpacks, black galoshes, flashlights, and each wears a necklace showing a different object that references the types of occupations held by these women, such as field laborer, midwife, gardener, and seamstress. Shimomura visualizes the idea of strangeness that immigrants felt, migrating to a new country with only vague familiarity with some Western sensibilities. As Asians, the immigrants bear "yellow" culture on their backs, wear galoshes to symbolize their journey over the Pacific Ocean, and wear Mickey Mouse ears to symbolize the fantasy of the America dream.

Shimomura uses Cinderella, another Disney fairytale character, to narrate the historical context behind the picture brides in his strategic form of parody because this historical event was nothing like a storybook romance [IMAGE 115].[66] A photograph of Yoshitomi Seibi Shimomura in 1912—Toku's future husband and Roger's grandfather—is projected on the slide screen as Cinderella enters the stage and states, "Without fear, she will meet her future husband, a missionary who has emigrated to America...How young she was...The moment the tape was cut for sailing, her dreams were interrupted by feelings of apprehension...She then parted from her father and mother to sail over the Pacific Ocean." Picture slides change back to Hokusai's *Wave*, and the dancers continue their immigration dance until a foghorn signals the end of the scene and the theater fades to black. Similar to the male immigrants, the female immigrants exhibited strength and sacrifice, leaving behind the comforts and resources of their families in order to emigrate to a new country in hopes of better futures. With only exchanged photographs and the help of a matchmaker (*omiai*), these women sailed across the Pacific Ocean, with no return ticket, to meet their husbands. The picture brides were a unique aspect of the Japanese American experience between 1908 and 1924, with approximately ten thousand Issei women becoming immigrant picture brides. This was the only way for Issei men to

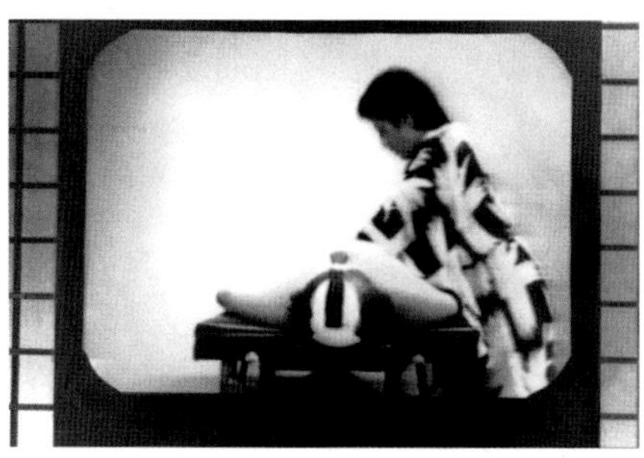

IMAGE 116: Detail (Photograph by Roger Shimomura, *The Last Sansei Story*, April 20, 1993, Haskell Indian Junior College: Lawrence, Kansas).

start a family in the United States; the Gentleman's Agreement Act of 1908 was an agreement negotiated between the U.S. and Japanese governments to put a stop to future Japanese male immigrant laborers, in return for supporting the large population of Issei bachelors through picture brides and the opportunity to have a family.

The Noh dancer, who has been frozen in the aisle, is reilluminated by a spotlight. She howls and walks approximately fifteen paces toward the stage before freezing in place to signal the next chapter of Toku's life. A picture slide showing the subtitle "Religion" and accompanied by the sound of a Japanese American man singing a cappella hymns in Japanese introduces Yoshitomi and his marriage through the picture-bride system to Toku. A video of a samurai being massaged by an Asian woman appears, creating the emotional tension of the soon-to-be-married couple. Shimomura strategically uses his art to discuss some of the perceived incongruences of the Japanese American experience by U.S. society, here juxtaposing the piety of religious values with the salacious notion of a massage as emblematic of his grandparent's union of marriage [IMAGE 116]. A kurogo enters holding a flashlight and communion tray and randomly selects an audience member to administer the body and blood of Christ using Wonder Bread and Welch's grape juice as slide projections of the Wonder Bread and Welch's juice appear for the audience members not offered communion to understand the symbolism of this unconventional perfomance theater experience [IMAGE 117]. As the picture slides switch to a telescopic view of war atrocities, Shimomura shows the human sacrifice of war fought for religious, political, and economic gain. This is another juxtaposition Shimomura uses to bring the audience's attention to issues of cultural morality and human sacrifice that are foundational principles of Christianity, Toku's chosen religion.

While these gruesome picture slides are shown, an Asian female performer wearing a choir robe and a bonnet-style hair dryer on her head is spotlit on stage and sings "Holy, Holy, Holy" [IMAGE 118]. On the second verse, two white crosses are projected side-by-side, and a teenage boy and girl representing Yoshitomi (Seibi) and Toku stand in front of each cross. On the third verse, the boy asks the girl to dance, and she agrees, presumably referring

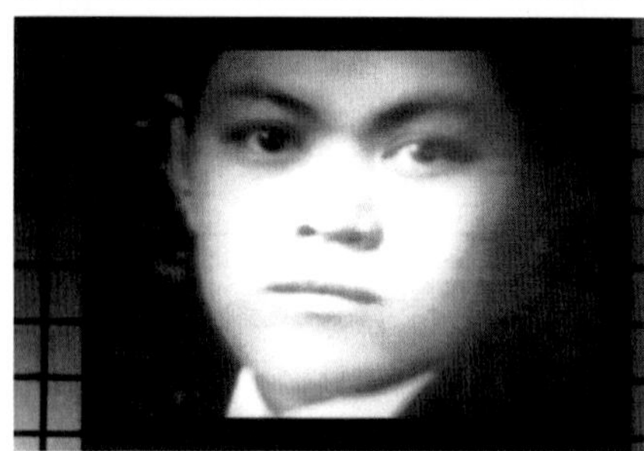

Top, IMAGE 117: Detail.

Center, IMAGE 118: Helen Cheng as Choir Girl.

Above left, IMAGE 119: Detail.

Above right, IMAGE 120: Detail.

Right, IMAGE 121: Detail.

(All photographs by Roger Shimomura, *The Last Sansei Story*, April 20, 1993, Haskell Indian Junior College: Lawrence, Kansas).

to Shimomura's grandparents' marriage. After the song, the choirgirl says, "Amen," and exits as the stage goes black. Shimomura uses symbolism pertaining to Christianity, war, marriage, and immigration to consider the motives, justifications, and sacrifices made by Japanese Americans, such as his grandparents, and to highlight major themes of the Japanese American experience.

A spotlight on the Noh dancer signals the next segment of act one, as he howls and takes fifteen more steps toward the stage. Then the audience sees a picture slide that reads, "Grandpa." On video, there are three photographs of Seibi Shimomura from early, middle, and old ages before fading to black [IMAGES 119-121]. Japanese popular music fades in and out, and a letter he wrote to his living relatives in Japan before he passed away in 1972 is read:

> *This is Seibi Shimomura. First I must apologize for not writing you. You have been very kind to me. Your letters and presents are precious reminders of my life in Japan, and I treasure them. Your parents selected Toku as my wife after a thorough search for a suitable spouse for me, and they sent Toku to me in America. I regret to tell you that I did not succeed economically as much as I should have in America, simply because I was an uneducated country boy. But as you know, success is not determined solely by money, and thanks to your parents, Toku and I have been quite happy together...*[67]

Using his grandfather's words to his relatives, Shimomura introduces Seibi's story and the importance of Toku in his life. The music shifts to flute, and two picture slides depicting an ukiyo-e country landscape with a samurai in the foreground appear, accompanied by Seibi the performer, dressed in 1920s American attire [IMAGE 122]. Seibi is aligned with the image of the samurai, and when the picture slide is illuminated, the American-dressed Seibi walks proudly forward and exits off-stage, symbolizing his emigration to the United States. The picture slides change to reveal an alley and backdoor. Now Seibi appears as a cook to the left of the stage, and voices yell, "Jap, go home! Jap, get out of here! Jap—" and so on as rocks are thrown at him [IMAGE 123]. Shimomura juxtaposes this racially charged experience with the dream of coming to America, emphasizing the discrimination and the political and economic difficulties Seibi faced to provide for his family.

Top, IMAGE 122: Laura Ramberg as Seibi; bottom, IMAGE 123: Detail (Photographs by Roger Shimomura, *The Last Sansei Story*, April 20, 1993, Haskell Indian Junior College: Lawrence, Kansas).

The picture slides change to journal notations from Seibi's diaries, written in Japanese, recording world events and their effects on the stock market. On the left, Seibi now sits in a chair reading the newspaper as a ticker tape is heard with a sudden crashing sound, symbolizing the stock market crash that threw the United States into the Great Depression [IMAGE 124]. Seibi slumps in his chair in a fit of depression as much of their savings was lost, as were most Americans' savings. The picture slide changes to a newspaper article of the Shimomuras' fiftieth wedding anniversary, and Seibi, still seated in his chair, listens to an audiotape of Toku recounting her life story [IMAGE 125]. Still depressed about the successes he was not fully able to accomplish, Seibi rips the tape from the cassette player. Seibi's angst is not with his marriage to Toku, but more with the outcome of his life. He wanted to be a dentist, but instead he eventually owned a small grocery store, and was forced to leave his business during incarceration and upon his release had to settle for being a janitor at a YWCA during the postwar period. Due

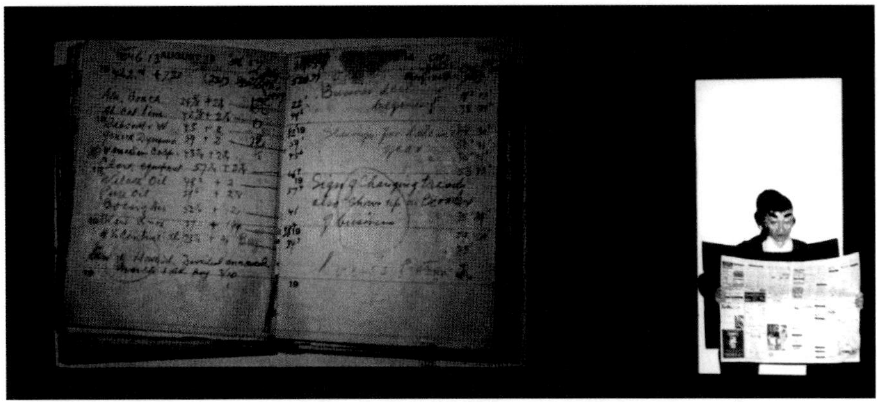

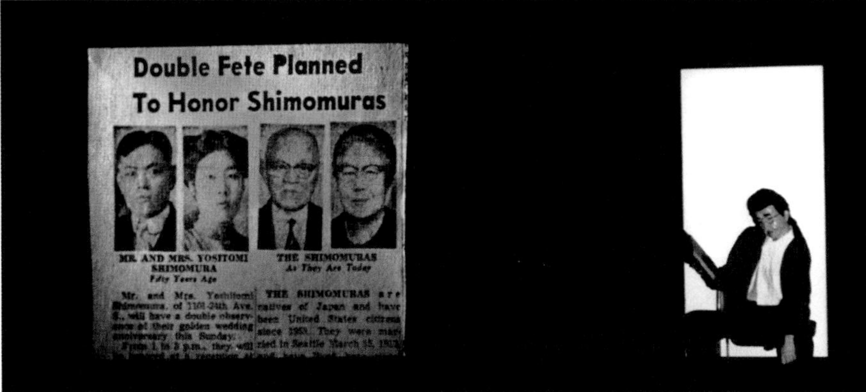

Top, IMAGE 124: Detail; Bottom, IMAGE 125: Detail (Photographs by Roger Shimomura, *The Last Sansei Story*, April 20, 1993, Haskell Indian Junior College: Lawrence, Kansas).

to events beyond his control (racism, the Great Depression, World War II, and the Japanese American incarceration), Seibi was never able to fulfill his goals. Seibi now appears with Alzheimer's disease, walking aimlessly around the stage and clapping his hands occasionally to kill imaginary flies [IMAGE 126]. The video depicting Seibi's photo from 1912 that he exchanged with Toku reappears, and a coffin is projected, bringing an end to Seibi's life. The hardship, discrimination, and challenges Seibi endured to build a better life for his children and grandchildren are a form of success worthy of celebration as part of America's history.

The Noh dancer is reilluminated for the final time. She howls and begins to walk toward the stage and out of the theater. Toku's voice is heard reciting the names of babies she delivered as a picture slide reading, "Grandma: The Midwife," is shown. Over the names of the babies, the audience hears audio of Toku reciting her biography:

IMAGE 126: Marsha Paludan as Seibi (Photograph by Roger Shimomura, *The Last Sansei Story*, April 20, 1993, Haskell Indian Junior College: Lawrence, Kansas).

> *In 1917 I took the [Washington] State examination for midwifery with twelve other Japanese, seven German, and three Italian applicants. The examination was held at a high school auditorium. We Japanese had an interpreter named Kakuichi Katayama, and we took a test consisting of 108 questions, lasting from 8:00 a.m. to 4:00 p.m. The test wasn't difficult as a whole, for we had actual experience. But in anatomy it was rather hard to remember what we had learned. Later I heard the examiner was amazed at the knowledge Japanese midwives showed, and it made me feel good. As I passed the examination, I added to my original title as "midwife licensed by the Japanese Ministry of Home Affairs" the new one, which read "licensed midwife in the State of Washington."*[68]

The video starts with a close-up of Toku at her nursing corps graduating class in Seattle, and then a sequence begins, fading in and out, of babies she delivered over the course of her career [IMAGE 127]. Toku helped deliver over one thousand babies, so the two slide projectors also alternate photographs of these babies over the duration of her midwife story. Toku continues to tell her story:

> *Up to this time, midwives were paid a gratuity only, following an old Japanese custom. So our income varied, sometimes from fifteen, to twenty or twenty-five dollars per delivery. After we were licensed in the State of Washington, we organized a union and the fee was set at thirty-five dollars. But some Japanese families couldn't afford to pay this amount. Midwives sometimes had to even provide clothing and diapers for babies. Some of the babies whose parents couldn't afford*

IMAGE 127: Toku and graduating class of midwives (Photograph by Roger Shimomura, *The Last Sansei Story*, April 20, 1993, Haskell Indian Junior College: Lawrence, Kansas)

> *to pay the midwife at the time of their birth are now taking active roles in the Japanese community. The babies I delivered and took care of have grown up and become doctors, officials, and professors. I wonder if any of them have ever thought of their old midwife who has watched them growing and prospering with tears of joy, as if they were her own children. In one month I had at most seven or eight babies to deliver. As I had no assistant and some families had no helping hands, I had young fathers help in preparing hot water and so on.*[69]

During this portion of the monologue, a kurogo passes out fifteen cards to audience members. The cards show pictures of babies Toku delivered, with typical Nisei names, such as "Hippo" Fujiyama, "Poison" Watanabe, and "Fuzzy" Sekijima [IMAGES 128-129]. Toku's impact on the Japanese American community is beyond measure, bringing over one thousand babies into this community. Like Seibi, it is the small acts that amount to prosperity, and that is not merely measured by personal economic gains.

As the video and picture slides come to an end, the background audio plays a ticking clock and the recitation of baby names fades. Then Toku says, "Four more minutes (pauses), three more minutes (pauses)," until the clock reaches midnight. Synchronized with Toku's timekeeping are picture slides of a clock at four minutes to twelve, then three, two, and one. At midnight, the video shows a close-up of Toku's diary entry on "June 26, 1939 (Roger's birthday)" and then fades out. The ticking stops, and in the silence the audience hears a baby's cry [IMAGE 130-31]. Toku begins to sing "Kadasu," a Japanese fairy-tale song, as a kurogo holding a long pole with a carp

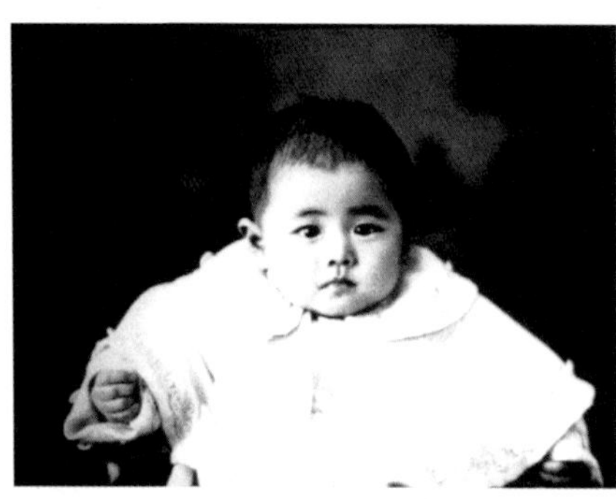

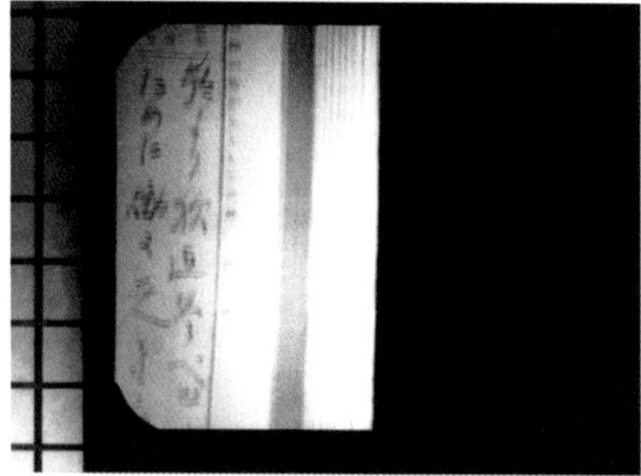

Top, IMAGE 128: Detail.

Center, left, IMAGE 129: Detail.

Center right 1, IMAGE 130: Detail.

Center right 2, IMAGE 131: Detail.

Bottom, IMAGE 132: Detail.

(All photographs by Roger Shimomura, *The Last Sansei Story*, April 20, 1993, Haskell Indian Junior College: Lawrence, Kansas).

windsock on the end (an iconic symbol for Children's Day in Japan), walks around the stage waving the pole until the song is over [IMAGE 132]. Toku ends the act with the final words *kodomo no tame ni,* meaning "for the sake of the children," to summarize the primary goal of the Issei.

Part Two: "The Nisei"

Part two, "The Nisei," was performed separately under the title *Campfire Diary*. When performed as part of *The Last Sansei Story*, the introduction reflects the same format as the other two acts of *The Last Sansei Story*. The set design of "The Nisei" opens with biparting walls of tarpaper barracks flanking a large video projection screen, accompanied by circus-type music. The video starts with a circus juggler dressed as a second-generation Japanese American, or Nisei, in a Hawaiian shirt with Japanese designs and juggling three objects—a baseball, a blond doll's head, and a *daruma* (good-luck charm). Off to the left of the stage, two slide projectors display—one slide with the title "The Nisei" and the adjacent picture slide showing the three symbolic Nisei objects. These objects symbolize the ratio of Americanness to Japaneseness that the Nisei, the second-generation Americans, embody: two-thirds American and one-third Japanese. The generational assimilation of Japanese Americans is a topic Shimomura illuminates for further discussion.

Shimomura also adds a new beginning to each diary entry to differentiate *The Last Sansei Story* from *Campfire Diary*, as another layer of symbolism and a historical marker of each new act, similar to the Noh dancer. Before each of the six diary entries is read in "The Nisei," Shimomura signals the next entry with dissonant chords and drums, along with a spotlight on his version of Lady Liberty shrouded in black. Dressed in a long gown, she holds a modern health (weight) scale, with a noose around her neck and headphones over her ears, and she walks slowly across the stage as a reminder of the injustice all Japanese Americans experienced during their incarceration [IMAGE 133].

Part Three: "The Sansei"

Part three, "The Sansei," opens with the same introduction of circus music and a video of a juggler, but now the panels are made from aluminum siding, symbolizing suburban America, and the juggler wears a baseball hat and Andy Warhol's Marilyn Monroe T-shirt, and he juggles a baseball,

IMAGE 133: Kari Paludan as Liberty. (Photograph by Roger Shimomura, *The Last Sansei Story*, April 20, 1993, Haskell Indian Junior College: Lawrence, Kansas).

a blond doll's head, and a Mickey Mouse doll. Off to the left, the title slide, "The Sansei," appears next to a picture slide of the three objects being juggled. These objects symbolize the ratio of Americanness to Japaneseness that the Sansei, meaning third-generation American, embody: three-thirds American culture and zero thirds Japanese culture. Then 1960s slow, bluesy jazz music begins, and a spotlight shows a performer dressed as a Black Panther Party member walking slowly across the stage, wearing headphones and snapping his fingers to the beat of the music [IMAGE 134]. Shimomura uses the Black Panther Party to signify the cultural shift in the United States sparked by the civil rights movement and the antigovernment protests for human equality by organizations like the Black Panther Party.

Once the Black Panther is off-stage, a video montage begins, starting with an Asian American girl practicing tap dance and accompanied by a pianist who plays "Tea for Two." The screen to the left of the video projection shows a picture slide of a football field. Periodically throughout the act, a performer dressed as a cheerleader, with a large "A" on her uniform and wearing an Asian mask, steps out enthusiastically onto the stage and yells through her cheer-phone, "Give me an A!" [IMAGE 135] Once the first stanza of "Tea for Two" is complete, a clapboard interrupts the videotaped dance practice with film stills of stereotypical portrayals of Asians and Asian Americans (for example, Bruce Lee in martial arts)—and often by non-Asian actors such as Sidney Toler (*Charlie Chan*), Marlon Brando (*The Teahouse of the August Moon*), Bob Hope (*Road to Hong Kong*), Shirley MacLaine (*My Geisha*)—each new example signaled by the clapboard.

Shimomura's message begins with the awkward cultural mixing that occurs when Japanese and U.S. cultures intermingle, and it moves on to the more subtle power dynamics and visual racism that occur by removing Asians from mainstream media and only offering stereotypical portrayals [IMAGES 136-37]. Furthermore, Shimomura is deconstructing stereotypes

IMAGE 134: Dwayne Lewis as Black Panther (Photograph by Roger Shimomura, *The Last Sansei Story*, April 20, 1993, Haskell Indian Junior College: Lawrence, Kansas).

that support racist and nationalist ideologies. On a personal note, Shimomura disclosed how he went to college with Bruce Lee and that Lee felt that the Chinese were superior to the Japanese—and that his martial art prowess and movies proved this point.[70] Shimomura does not support this type of nationalist and racist thinking. All the while, Shimomura keeps the performance hyped with a cheerleader calling, "Give me an A!" to reflect yet another stereotype of Asian Americans as the model minority. Although the model minority is a more "positive" stereotype, its danger lies in assuming that all Asian Americans are the same—successful and prosperous, and not suffering from poverty, discrimination, and unequal distribution of resources. All of these themes are relevant to the Japanese American experience, and Shimomura deliberately leaves the door open for conversation.

IMAGE 135: Cheerleader (Photograph by Roger Shimomura, *The Last Sansei Story*, April 20, 1993, Haskell Indian Junior College: Lawrence, Kansas).

Shimomura adds another layer of meaning through audience participation, as during the montage, Kurogo 1 passes three trays of origami boxes to audience members as gifts that aid in the transfer of meaning from performance to viewer. Inside each box is a message from Toku that describes

IMAGE 136: Detail and IMAGE 137: Detail, (Photograph by Roger Shimomura, *The Last Sansei Story*, April 20, 1993, Haskell Indian Junior College: Lawrence, Kansas).

advice Roger received as a child from his grandmother, along with a piece of Japanese candy. The first tray of boxes states, "Grandma always said, 'Everything you do, good or bad, will reflect upon the entire Japanese race.'" Kurogo 1 departs and reenters with a second tray of boxes; however, this time the message states, "Grandma always said, 'Always do more than is expected of you.'" The third tray states, "Grandma always said, 'Don't stand out in a crowd. People will notice you.'" These are subtle, intimate, and deeply personal messages transmitted between Shimomura and his grandmother. They reveal values of the Shimomura family as well as U.S. cultural perceptions.

Shimomura adds this layer of "subtextual" information to selected audience members, hoping they will share the information with one another and push the boundaries of performance art by becoming directive members of the performance.[71] He recodes and passes on his memories, and advice that he may or may not have taken, allowing his audience to understand the values the Issei wanted to pass down to their children and grandchildren, and also the irony of how unlike the messages his art must be. In the context of *The Last Sansei Story*, this artistic device demonstrates how history can be lost and memories forgotten, and how a cultural identity transforms and may even cease to exist, as the audience members did not circulate these messages and gifts that the artist provided. Shimomura shared his experience—specifically, the values of how to conduct himself in U.S. society—to expand the types of topics surrounding the Japanese American experience. Here are a few questions that are raised by the performance: Are the Sansei still connected to Japan? Is doing more than what is expected of you a Japanese sensibility? What benefit comes from staying invisible? What

IMAGE 138: Kentaro Fukada as Stereotyped Other (Photograph by Roger Shimomura, *The Last Sansei Story*, April 20, 1993, Haskell Indian Junior College: Lawrence, Kansas).

does this say about the position of Japanese Americans in U.S. society?

When the audio reaches the end of the second stanza of "Tea for Two," a song title that implies a meeting of two people (two cultures), the music of the dance rehearsal changes to "Anything Goes," a symbolic pun to the odd and questionable cultural mixing that Shimomura is highlighting. To emphasize the point, Shimomura adds a performer wearing a Chinese mask and Japanese kimono and performing a mock tap dance in front of the videotaped rehearsal across the entire stage. This performance concludes with the cheerleader appearing and shouting, "Give me an A!" [IMAGE 138]

The music changes back to the introductory 1960s bluesy jazz with the spotlight on the Black Panther performer snapping his fingers and listening to his music, signaling the end of the segment and the start of a new historical moment. Shimomura now inserts a personal vignette. The picture slides now depict Shimomura as a boy playing war with his two childhood friends, and the audio changes to an argument between children: "You be the Jap." "No, you be the Jap." "No, I always have to be the Jap. It's your turn" [IMAGE 139]. Shimomura applies all of these facets of his multimedia performance art—the stereotypical and nonexistent presence of Asian Americans in mainstream media, the model minority stereotype, the values passed down to their children, the lack of sociohistorical awareness of the Japanese American experience, and the awkward cultural mixings that resonated in the artist's life—to the innocent childhood play and emotions of always playing, and being seen as, the "Jap."

IMAGE 139: Detail (Photograph by Roger Shimomura, *The Last Sansei Story*, April 20, 1993, Haskell Indian Junior College: Lawrence, Kansas).

The next scene opens with a video projection showing a 1950s couple dancing the cha-cha, but it focuses only on the two sets of feet. Frankie Avalon's "Venus" plays as a video shows the mission statement for "Valeda," an all Japanese American sorority at the University of Washington, followed by picture slides of the Valeda members from Shimomura's college yearbook [IMAGE 140]. On stage, six performers—three boys and three girls—appear, wearing Asian masks and mortarboards for graduation and carrying hubcaps—a favored item of Shimomura's to collect from cars in the 1950s. After their entrance poses—girls gossiping and acting coy, guys posing and mugging—they dance the cha-cha and eventually assemble themselves into a car shape and dance and wave as they exit the stage to the end of "Venus" [IMAGE 141].

Then, the Shirelles' "Soldier Boy" begins, and two white crosses are projected, illuminating an Asian-masked girl performer and a life-sized Superman doll. The second verse begins, and they start to slow dance, unilluminating

IMAGE 140: Detail (Photograph by Roger Shimomura, *The Last Sansei Story*, April 20, 1993, Haskell Indian Junior College: Lawrence, Kansas).

Top, IMAGE 141: College Students; Left, IMAGE 142: Detail; Right, IMAGE 143: Detail (All photographs by Roger Shimomura, *The Last Sansei Story*, April 20, 1993, Haskell Indian Junior College: Lawrence, Kansas).

one of the crosses. As she pulls out the air stop from the inflatable Superman while continuing to dance, three male performers return to the stage and enter the audience area, inviting audience members to dance with them. By the third verse, Superman is completely deflated in her arms [IMAGES 142-43]. She continues dancing with him, moving off the stage into the audience, and then all four performers exit the theater at the end of the song. Kurogo 1 returns with another tray of boxes, stating, "Grandmother always said, 'Don't outwardly show how you feel about things.'" Shimomura draws from his college experience, in which certain cultural influences are accepted into U.S. culture, while others remain segregated, and even when cultural mixing occurs, it is superficial, imaginary, and short-lived, as Superman is not a real dance partner. Toku's advice of not externally showing how you feel internally is a defense mechanism and does not aid in solving racial inequality.

Then a video of Dan "Boy" Wildcat,[72] a professor at Haskell Indian Nations University, wearing a cowboy hat, playing the guitar, and singing while sitting on the toilet is shown. After the first verse, a Sansei song leader enters the stage and encourages the audience to sing along using their song sheets. He is dressed in street clothes and a backward baseball hat, and he bounces a red ball while Kurogo 2 blows bubbles at him, perhaps in reference to Do Ho's song "Tiny Bubbles" in part two, "The Nisei." Then, the Sansei performer sings the second verse of the original song by Dan "Boy" Wildcat titled "Yellow All Same."

Maki-sushi, Sukiyaki,
Chow Mein, sushi balls,
Egg foo yung—they're oriental.
Mr. Moto, Hirohito,
Bruce Lee, and Hop Sing,
It don't matter, yellow all the same.

(Chorus)

Yellow all the same, what's in a name?
Yellow all the same, yin is the game.

kimchi, miso, Da Nang, Ming sho,
Mazda, and dim sum,
Ho Chi Min [Minh] and Kim Park Lee Yung,

Shimomura, Dalai Lama,
Godzilla, and Kong,
It don't matter if the name is all wrong.

(Chorus)

Vo Nguyen Jopp [Giap], geeshee bar hop,
Ninja, Sun Yung [Myung] Moon,
Siam Prince and houseboy, monsoon,

Singapore Sling, Connie Chung King,
Ying-and-Yang thang,
It don't matter; yellow all same.

IMAGE 144: Detail (Photograph by Roger Shimomura, *The Last Sansei Story*, April 20, 1993, Haskell Indian Junior College: Lawrence, Kansas).

(Chorus)

(Chorus)[73]

The song was inspired by Shimomura's earlier performance in *California Sushi* of the same title that pointed out differences between Japanese and Chinese culture in an effort to elevate cultural sensitivity to difference. Here, however, the desire to educate viewers of cultural differences is gone, and the lack of cultural awareness for difference is highlighted through an awkward tension between racism and frivolity.

Once the song ends, the video changes to a portrayal of a Japanese American girl watching TV while eating a salad with chopsticks [IMAGE 144]. Melodic music begins, and picture slides alternate every three seconds, showing corporate brand logos while "On Buying American," written by Dan Wildcat, is recited:

The Toyota Camry is built in Kentucky by Americans.
The Mazda 626 is built in Michigan.
The Nissan Sentra is built in Tennessee.
Toyota Corolla cars and Toyota pickups are built in California.

The Geo Metro is imported from Japan.
John Deere earthmovers are built in Japan.
Komatsu earthmovers are built in America.
The Ford Probe is built in Michigan by Mazda.
The Dodge Stealth is made in Nagoya, Japan.
The Plymouth Laser is built in Illinois by Mitsubishi.
The Geo Prism is built in California by Toyota.
GM owns 37 percent of Isuzu.
Ford owns 25 percent of Mazda.[74]

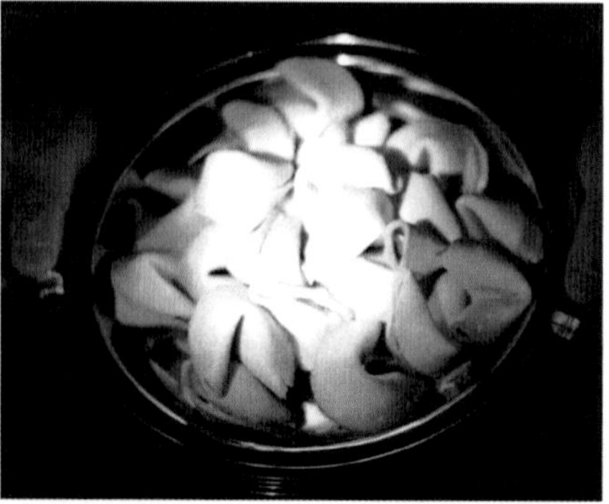

Left, IMAGE 145 and right, IMAGE 146: Details (Photographs by Roger Shimomura, *The Last Sansei Story*, April 20, 1993, Haskell Indian Junior College: Lawrence, Kansas).

Shimomura and Wildcat outline the interconnected global economy of these large corporations and demonstrate how "American" brands are made in Japan, and "Japanese" brands are made in the United States [IMAGE 145]. During the 1990s there was a recession, and American auto manufacturers purchased foreign auto companies, while foreign auto manufacturers built factories in the United States. The push to buy "American-made" vehicles spurred racial tensions and resulted in random acts of violence, such as the death of Vincent Chin in 1992, a Chinese American man who was beaten to death by two Caucasian U.S. auto-industry workers because they thought he was Japanese. [75] Shimomura shows how the seemingly innocuous idea of "buying American" is not so simple and that it fuels stereotypical ideas and racist sentiments against Asians and Asian Americans.

During the video, picture slides, and reading of "On Buying American," Kurogo 1 enters the auditorium again with a new tray to hand out to audience members, this time passing out fortune cookies with a message inside stating, "Fortune cookies are not Japanese" [IMAGE 146]. Again, Shimomura raises the notion of cultural sensitivity of difference—but at a subtextual level, as not every member of the audience receives this gift, reinforcing the need for greater cultural sensitivity of difference.

As this segment of the Sansei experience fades to black, the 1960s rhythmic jazz music begins, and the Black Panther performer snaps his fingers to the music in his headphones and walks across the stage for the final time. On the video screen is a close-up pan across all the misspellings of Shimomura's name over the last ten years from his mail [IMAGE 147]. The audio is of

Shimomura's voice attempting to pronounce each misspelling. As the video and audio progress, Shimomura's voice is overlaid, and the pronunciations of his name become increasingly unrecognizable, while the cheerleader's voice is heard in the background yelling, "Give me an A!" Shimomura highlights the irony of the model minority being so minor that surnames are "too foreign" and are rendered unrecognizable. As Shimomura's experience is symbolic of *The Last Sansei Story*, his name, like his history and his connection to Japan, literally becomes indecipherable.

The concluding scene of the performance verges on the burlesque. Shimomura's humor and sarcasm escalate as he pushes the boundaries of art. Slow, sleazy, honky-tonk music begins, and the video shows an obese performer wearing a Caucasian face mask, kimono, feather boa, and pearls, smoking a cigarette and walking ungracefully and inappropriately toward the camera [IMAGE 148]. As the music increases in intensity, the camera zooms to a close-up on the woman's masked face. The parodied woman symbolizes an overindulgent, classless, and self-aggrandizing person. Shimomura creates this parody as a metaphoric mirror of the appearance of cultural insensitivity in U.S. perceptions and attitudes. As the video fades

IMAGE 147: Detail (Photographs by Roger Shimomura, *The Last Sansei Story*, April 20, 1993, Haskell Indian Junior College: Lawrence, Kansas).

IMAGE 148: Kari Paludan as Stereotyped American (Photographs by Roger Shimomura, *The Last Sansei Story*, April 20, 1993, Haskell Indian Junior College: Lawrence, Kansas).

to black, the two slide projectors show a Kansas landscape, and the obscene female performer steps on stage and moves raunchily around before walking up the aisle, engaging audience members as she goes, before exiting out the back. The picture slide changes to "The End" and *The Last Sansei Story* comes to an abrupt close; the only trace of Japanese culture is the kimono.

The Last Sansei Story is an unprecedented piece of performance art that offers historical documentation of primary resources pertaining to the Japanese American experience blended with Americana and U.S. popular culture. Shimomura covers ninety years of Japanese American history and raises several topics of importance surrounding race relations, identity, and U.S. history. Shimomura states that *The Last Sansei Story* is not an attempt "to offer a definitive dialogue on the Japanese Americans."[76] *The Last Sansei Story* is one artistic attempt to address the unparalleled historical circumstances and unique characteristics of a group of people—from Shimomura's interpretation. The arist hopes that *The Last Sansei Story* raises awareness and sparks a dialogue about the Japanese American experience and that there will be more conversations, artworks, and emergent stories to follow.

Detail (Photograph by Roger Shimomura, *Yellow Potluck/ Fortune Cookies Are Not Japanese*, July 5-7, 1994, 205 West Forty-Second Street: New York City, New York).

8 yellow potluck/fortune cookies are not japanese

- **Installation: 205 West Forty-Second Street, New York, New York, July 5 to September 5, 1994**
- **Performance: 205 West Forty-Second Street, New York, New York, July 5-7, 1994**

Shimomura was one of twenty-five artists, architects, and designers invited by *Creative Time*, New York, to participate in the Forty-Second Street Art Project that created round-the-clock art installations and galleries to make over Manhattan's Times Square.[77] The gentrification effort transformed a seedy area overrun with pornographic stores into businesses offering wholesome family entertainment. Over the two-month period, artists were invited to create temporary, site-specific installations. It was estimated that over one million people viewed the Forty-Second Street Art Project.

Yellow Potluck is an installation at 205 West Forty-Second Street, New York, New York, inside the storefront windows of a former U.S. retail store, from July 5 to September 5, 1994. On July 5, *Fortune Cookies Are Not Japanese*, written and directed by Shimomura and performed by Kwang Yu Fong, was performed at the *Yellow Potluck* installation. Both artistic pieces comment on the complexities of multiculturalism, which was a timely topic, as the 1993 Whitney Museum of American Art Biennial was a momentous (and controversial) step toward showcasing artists of color in a keystone American art institution. The Whitney Biennial addressed the subject of multiculturalism, as up until that point, the institution had shown fewer than ten percent of artists of color, reflecting a disconnect with the U.S. demographic and cultural makeup.[78] Multiculturalism speaks to greater visibility of the plurality of cultures from different ethnic backgrounds who comprise the U.S. citizenry.

Importantly, *Yellow Potluck/Fortune Cookies Are Not Japanese* presents a critical dialogue on the topic of multiculturalism. Shimomura questions the hard-fought visibility and pluralism that multiculturalism offers, and he digs into the complexities of this topic through three lenses: first, racially, being

IMAGE 150: Detail (Photograph by Roger Shimomura, *Yellow Potluck/Fortune Cookies Are Not Japanese*, July 5-7, 1994, 205 West Forty-Second Street: New York City, New York).

seen as or viewing all Asian and Asian Americans as similar (the idea that all Asians look the same); second, politically, in solidarity as a united Asian American identity (Asian and Pacific American coalitions); and, third, culturally, Asian Americans coming from divergent cultural backgrounds that go unrecognized.

From the street, the left display case of *Yellow Potluck* features Western-style architecture symbolized through a brick wall with a window in the foreground [IMAGE 150]. To engage the viewer, Shimomura uses a male mannequin, leaning out from behind the wall, whose face is painted using Kabuki makeup but who wears a Western, button-up, collared dress shirt. As he awaits the arrival of his female companion, presumably for dinner, a hibachi-style grill is ready to cook the Japanese-style meal in front of the western-style brick wall with an electric rice cooker nearby leading the viewer's eye down and to the right to the edge of the wall. Shimomura engineered the installation so the interior space could be easily viewed from the street [IMAGE 151]. Peering behind an exterior wall to the interior, viewers see off to the right a shoji with silhouettes of a Japanese couple copulating, while behind the brick wall, to the left, is a table set with a steak dinner, potatoes, vegetables, and chopsticks [IMAGE 152].

The images Shimomura draws from for the silhouettes and the framed print hanging over the dinner table are ukiyo-e and shunga. Shimomura's print "Match, No Mix" features two couples kissing: first, an ukiyo-e, shunga-style couple, and, second, a U.S. comic book couple [IMAGE 153]. While compositionally the two couples match, ethnically and culturally, they do not mix. The entire installation is a carefully crafted mixing of Japanese and American culture. The sexual undertones of Shimomura's *Yellow Potluck* acknowledge the previous characteristic of the neighborhood but through the lens of the Japanese American experience. *Yellow Potluck* examines the contradiction of U.S. cultural values, such as democracy, equality, freedom of expression, and a touting of its cultural diversity, yet the need for movements such as multiculturalism and identity politics demonstrates the imbalances and existence of institutional racism, lack of cultural diversity, inequality, and injustice that continue to affect people of color.

Top left, IMAGE 151: Detail; top right, IMAGE 152: Detail; bottom right, IMAGE 153: Detail.

(All photographs by Roger Shimomura, *Yellow Potluck/Fortune Cookies Are Not Japanese*, July 5-7, 1994, 205 West Forty-Second Street: New York City, New York).

The right display case of *Yellow Potluck* uses the same architectural format of a brick wall in the foreground and a shoji in the interior [IMAGE 154]. However, a Caucasian female mannequin poses in front of the brick wall wearing a geisha wig, kimono, high heels, and fur collar, with a transparent bag at her feet filled full of World War II publications featuring racist references and toys using stereotypical portrayals of Asians. The interior space shows a backlit shoji with a silhouetted lava lamp standing proudly in a phallic gesture on a table [IMAGE 155]. In front of the screen is a dining table set with a plate of sushi and a fork and knife, and above the table is a black-and-white family photograph of Shimomura as a toddler with his parents, standing in front of their communal barracks as incarcerated prisoners at Minidoka in Hunt, Idaho [IMAGE 156-57].

Shimomura finds meaning in each element he exhibits in the *Yellow Potluck* installation. The artist careful arranges the objects and subject matter through several layers of accessibility, to force the viewer to become cognizant of the Gaze and its unrecognized power and privilege on a public street into a private space. Comparing the two sides of *Yellow Potluck*, the female on the right side showcases the accepted forms of cultural appropriation of Japanese culture, food, dress, and design but highlights the historic and

Left, IMAGE 154 and right, IMAGE 155: Details (Photographs by Roger Shimomura, *Yellow Potluck/Fortune Cookies Are Not Japanese*, July 5-7, 1994, 205 West Forty-Second Street: New York City, New York).

Top, IMAGE 156: Detail; bottom, IMAGE 157: Detail.

(Photographs by Roger Shimomura, *Yellow Potluck/Fortune Cookies Are Not Japanese*, July 5-7, 1994, 205 West Forty-Second Street: New York City, New York).

IMAGE 158: Kwang Yu Fong (Photograph by Roger Shimomura, *Yellow Potluck/Fortune Cookies Are Not Japanese*, July 5-7, 1994, 205 West Forty-Second Street: New York City, New York).

racist attitudes as symbolized through the Japanese American incarceration and racist toys and publications. The male on the left side is interpreted as the assimilation of Japanese Americans to Western society. Japanese Americans are seen as Other, despite being U.S. citizens, speaking English as a first language, wearing American clothes, eating American food, and having few to no direct connections to Japan.

Kwang Yu Fong, a Peking Chinese Opera actor and performance artist, performed *Fortune Cookies Are Not Japanese* for three days at the *Yellow Potluck* installation. The performance opens to Chinese opera music. Kwang enters backward through the door separating the two window installations, riding a pretend horse. Her face is painted in Chinese opera makeup, and she wears casual street attire, jeans, and a Pink Floyd T-shirt [IMAGE 158]. Using Chinese-opera-style dance movements, she relates to objects inside the two display windows of the *Yellow Potluck* installation before engaging the audience by handing out fortune cookies that say, "Fortune cookies are not Japanese," and buttons that say, "Yellow all same" and "Yellow no same." Kwang also has these buttons pinned on her T-shirt. Once all the buttons are passed out, she resumes her Chinese-opera-style dancing for a few more minutes before exiting through the same door.

Fortune Cookies Are Not Japanese showcases the awkward cultural mixing among Asian and U.S. cultures as one aspect of the Asian American experience. Shimomura presents these oddities, symbolized through music, clothing, food, and dance, to simulate some of the obstacles and complexities of becoming part of U.S. society while maintaining elements of Asian cultural heritage. Shimomura uses the gifts to the audience to adjudicate cultural perceptions regularly encountered by Asian Americans—such as confusing Japanese for Chinese or Korean or Vietnamese or Filipino or Pacific Islander—in hopes of fostering a greater awareness of cultural sensitivity to difference. Labels—such as "Caucasian," "Western," "European," "Black," "African," "Asian," and "Hispanic"—define large geographic regions and physiological features. Confusing a German for a Spanish, English, Italian, Swiss, or French national would be a similar conflation of cultural difference. Ironically, and precisely to the point, fortune cookies are not Chinese, either. The fortune cookie has neither historical meaning nor precedent in Chinese culture and is a faux, branded, commoditized U.S. interpretation of Asian culture. Symbolically, the fortune cookie represents exactly the type of cultural assumption that, as a pop artist, Shimomura wants the audience to reevaluate.

Detail (Photograph by Roger Shimomura, *Songs for a Rickshaw Boy*, January 13, 1996, Spencer Art Museum, University of Kansas: Lawrence, Kansas).

9 songs for a rickshaw boy

- **Spencer Art Museum, University of Kansas, Lawrence, Kansas, January 13, 1996**
- **Western Gallery, Western Washington University, Bellingham, Washington, October 3, 1996**
- **Newcomb Art Gallery, Woldenberg Art Center, Newcomb College, Tulane University, New Orleans, Louisiana, January 25, 1997**

***Songs for a Rickshaw Boy* was first performed in conjunction with *Delayed Reaction*, a twenty-five-year retrospective, at the Spencer Museum of Art, the University of Kansas, on January 13, 1996. Included in this show were Shimomura's paintings, prints, installations, and performance work. This performance specifically focused on the ironies, complexities, and limitations of biculturalism of the Japanese American experience. This is one topic addressed and highlighted throughout Shimomura's multidisciplined retrospective.**

Broken into four sections over the two-hour reception, *Songs for a Rickshaw Boy* uses music, costume, and props to reflect a U.S. female's increasingly desperate attempts to acculturate to Japanese culture as a counterportrayal of the Japanese American experience. Shimomura stylizes the piece through the lens of pop culture with inflections of humor, absurdity, shock, sarcasm, and entertainment to capture the audience's attention using his signature style. The format of *Songs for a Rickshaw Boy* consists of the vocalist and performer Kelley Hunt, whose costumes and songs reflect her attempt to acculturate to Japanese culture, and a kurogo who follows her, passing out trays of various cultural markers that parallel the attempt at acculturation.

Thirty minutes into the reception, Hunt enters the gallery singing, "A Lovely Way to Spend an Evening," a 1943 pop classic with music by Jimmy McHugh and lyrics by Harold Adamson that was perhaps most famously sung by Frank Sinatra. Hunt wears a Kappa Kappa Gamma T-shirt, miniskirt, and high heels, and she sings into a wireless microphone. As Hunt moves around the gallery singing, she is followed by a kurogo passing a tray full of sushi and peanut butter finger sandwiches to the crowd. Her costume portrays Hunt as a Caucasian college student, while the Japanese and American food pairing is a subtle metaphor for the stark differences between Japanese and American culture; this is a tension that is present throughout Shimomura's art. After Hunt has completed "A Lovely Way to Spend an Evening," the kurogo places a translucent black cloth over her head, and they exit together.

Fifty-five minutes into the reception, Hunt and the kurogo return, this time singing and dancing to "I've Got You under My Skin," a song that won an Academy Award in 1936, written by Cole Porter with music by Nelson Riddle and most famously rerecorded by Frank Sinatra. Hunt adds to her attire a blond wig as a symbol of her attempt to acculturate into U.S. society. The kurogo passes out origami cranes folded in Japanese paper and Walt Disney-themed wrapping paper—the two types of paper reflecting the two countries, Japan and the United States. Once the song is completed, the kurogo places a translucent black cloth over her head, and they exit together. U.S. cultural acceptance of these hit songs over several generations is a successful cultural process that Shimomura deliberately highlights. Furthermore, "I've Got You under My Skin" is about an undeniable affair bringing together two disparate people and is a metaphor for Japanese and American culture differences.

Eighty minutes into the reception, Hunt and the kurogo return, singing "Come On to My House," a 1951 hit sung by Rosemary Clooney and written by Ross Bagdasarian and William Saroyan, which is based on an Armenian folk melody. The lyrics of the song are more campy where the invitation begins with giving candy and ultimately concludes with "I'm going to give you everything, everything, everything." All three songs focus on a relationship that is becoming increasingly serious, moving from a date and kiss, to an undeniable desire and attraction through an affair, and now to commitment of "everything"—suggestive of a sexual encounter or literally all of herself. Hunt adds a kimono to her costume, symbolizing her attempt to acculturate to Japanese culture and a more intimate attire, while the kurogo carries a tray of sake with four small cups and a bottle of wine with four wine glasses, again showcasing the differences between Japan and the United States. Once the song is completed, the kurogo places a translucent black cloth over her head, and they exit together.

An hour and forty-five minutes into the retrospective's reception, Hunt sings, "Hawaiian Wedding Song," and adds a geisha wig over her blond wig and actual hair, while the kurogo passes a tray of wedding packets of two kinds of rice—short and long grain rice—symbolizing Japanese and Chinese culture, respectively. "Hawaiian Wedding Song" was written by Charles King in 1926 as "Ke Kali Nei Au" and translated in 1958 by Al Hoffman and Dick Manning. Symbolically, Hunt's acculturation is complete as two become one through marriage, although it is clear with the use of short and long grain rice that the cultural differences between Japan and China are not completely understood. Hunt's costume is a layered, ridiculous combination that literally does not fit, but Shimomura is optimistically articulating how love is "blind" and infinite.

Shimomura's title of the performance, *Songs for a Rickshaw Boy*, is another ironic layer the artist gives to the performance, commenting on the cultural intersection of individualism verses communism. *Rickshaw Boy* is a 1941 Chinese literary classic influenced by Russia's communist ideology. The main character of the book struggles with the decision to be an owner and self-employed rickshaw boy—a free, independent person as a metaphor for democracy—or becoming a servant for someone else's family, symbolizing socialist society and serving China. The title is also a powerful metaphor for identity through the lens of individualism and having a choice to be and to be seen as whomever you determine.

Keiko Kira as Roger (Photograph by Roger Shimomura, *A Decade of Performances...Not Made in Japan*, February 1, 1996, Spencer Art Museum, University of Kansas: Lawrence, Kansas).

10 a decade of performances... not made in japan

- **Spencer Art Museum, University of Kansas, Lawrence, Kansas, February 1, 1996**
- **Western Gallery, Western Washington University, Bellingham, Washington, November 9, 1996**

A Decade of Performances...Not Made in Japan **was a hybrid lecture-performance that Shimomura created to commemorate his ten years of performance art. Instead of giving a traditional speech for receiving the forty-seventh Distinguished Professor Award from the University of Kansas on February 1, 1996, Shimomura elected to create a performance that he would perform to address not only his body of work over the past decade but also his less well-known interest in performance art stemming back to his master's thesis. Like most of his multimedia performances, Shimomura crafts each detail of his performance art to convey the pathos of the Japanese American experience. Shimomura uses performers, vocalists, and kurogos, and he blends U.S. and Japanese pop culture, music, and theater; creates custom audio tracks, costumes, picture slides, and videos; and incorporates the audience into the performance.**

A Decade of Performances...Not Made in Japan opens with a dark room and dimly lit performer standing at the lecture podium, dressed as a fisherman holding a fishing pole. The podium is red with the number twenty-six, symbolizing the pier from which Shimomura departed on his annual king salmon fishing outing at Point No Point, Washington. The sounds of ocean surf and seagulls are heard while picture slides of Point No Point are projected onto the screen, rotating every two minutes. The performer continues to reel in the line, checks it for fish, and then casts out the line. Among one to two hundred fishermen, each in sixteen-foot boats being pulled by the fast-moving current and seeking the prized king salmon, Shimomura describes this event as a performance in itself, paralleling the format of *A Decade of Performance Art*, as a lecture inside a performance.[79]

Shimomura enters the stage opposite the performer, turns on a lamp, and takes a seat. Paralleling Shimomura's actions, the performer turns off the lamp, the ocean sounds fade, and he exits the stage. Shimomura begins his monologue with the impetus for his decade of performance art. He states, "It seriously started in 1984, when I thought it would be nice to own a video camera in order to make my home video version of "Champion Fishing with Bill Dance." A picture slide of Bill Dance is projected, and the audience learns that the fisherman is emblematic of Shimomura and his yearly fishing trip with his children, starting at five in the morning. Like most video camera owners, Shimomura wanted to capture cherished family moments, but the medium of video was not new to Shimomura.

The picture slide changes to a photograph of Shimomura performing his master's thesis and a video segment of the film he created, titled *Back*, a faux Andy Warhol 16 mm film that Shimomura "discovered" at the New York Public Library, is projected on the screen. During his graduate thesis for the master of art at Syracuse University, Shimomura similarly presented a lecture-performance piece, titled *Andy Warhol and the Pop Culture*. In his monologue for *A Decade of Performances*, Shimomura describes that he fabricated an exclusive interview with Warhol to support the authenticity of the film. Importantly, Shimomura explains that he learned a valuable lesson about the power of performance art and its ability to create "reality" and change perceived notions of fact and fiction. He states, "Everyone believed what they heard and learned more than they realized about Andy Warhol, but I learned something even more about performance art." Shimomura, like Warhol, creates art inspired by U.S. popular culture and questions notions of authenticity, institutional power, authorship, cultural morality, branding, commodification, and art. However, unlike Warhol, Shimomura's work addresses the Japanese American experience.

A picture slide of Shimomura teaching his first design class at the University of Kansas, in 1972, is projected. Explaining the photograph, Shimomura describes that he accepted his first teaching position as an assistant professor of art at the University of Kansas and simultaneously made small headway through the Design Department teaching basic 3-D design in an attempt to incorporate aspects of performance art into freshman classes. As the lecture continues, Shimomura states that unfortunately, the potential of performance art to challenge the boundary between fiction and reality, and the financial commitment and sheer size of the computer-based equipment during the 1970s, were not considered priorities of either department's curriculum, so Shimomura focused on painting and would not use film again as a medium for another twelve years.

The video projection now shows Shimomura and Paludan's collaborative experimentations with students in Shimomura's studio, in 1984. Shimomura's lecture returns to his purchase of a video camera in 1984 and meeting choreographer and dancer Marsha Paludan at the Kansas University Gallery fall faculty show. The picture slide changes to Shimomura's *Diary Series* paintings (1983) and video of his first performance art piece, *Toku's Dance*, accompanied by low audio of the performance's music. Shimomura describes that after meeting Paludan and discussing his interest in developing the content of his paintings through the medium of film, Paludan and two or three dancers would meet every Wednesday evening at Shimomura's studio and be filmed. Together they would experiment through movement, costume, and masks with the implied events before and after the frozen moment of one of Shimomura's paintings. The videotaped experimentations quickly led to the first performance, titled *Toku's Dance*, with Paludan performing as Toku and thus beginning a long history of collaboration between Shimomura and Paludan.

As more picture slides from Shimomura's *Diary Series* paintings are shown, Shimomura enumerates a second significant collaboration, this time between himself and Jim Stringer, the director of sound for Centron (Film) Corporation. Continuing his lecture, Shimomura describes that he was invited by the Music Department to collaborate with a composer on a short performance piece for the Symposium of Contemporary Music at the University Theater. Stringer was significant in adding custom, hybrid soundscapes—another dimension of Shimomura's performance art that, like his paintings, would draw from popular U.S. and Japanese songs as well as evoke the cacophonous differences between U.S. and Japanese cultures to connote the merging of two very different cultures, thus reflecting the Japanese American experience.

After the audience hears a sampling of the audio composition from the *Seven Kabuki Plays Project*, picture slides of the *Diary Series* paintings and photographs of the corresponding act from the *Seven Kabuki Plays Project* resume. Shimomura continues his lecture and explains that the first act of the *Seven Kabuki Plays Project* was a fourteen-minute performance derived from Toku Shimomura's recently translated diary entries, specifically focusing on the Pearl Harbor attack by Japan and the subsequent incarceration of Japanese Americans. After separately performing what were to become the first and then second acts of the *Seven Kabuki Plays Project*, Shimomura states that he removed the self-imposed requirement of guiding the performance through a similar composition as his corresponding painting.

Suddenly, Kurogo 1 uses a clacker, which usually signals the start of each act, but here signals Kurogo 2's cue to enter the back of the theater and run down the aisle with a pitcher of water and a glass, setting both down in front of Shimomura before exiting the same way, but now to rapid clacking by Kurogo 1. Shimomura uses the concept of a kurogo in his performance art as a formal strategy that parallels his use of ukiyo-e and a traditional form of Japanese popular culture, as a mechanism to symbolize and foster dialogue about the Japanese American experience. Shimomura also choreographed this "interruption" to signal a break in the rules of both performance art and Western theater, and his performances would continue to break rules from this moment forward.

A kurogo gives away a copy of the *Seven Kabuki Plays Project* storyboard to an audience member, and Shimomura continues his lecture. Shimomura articulates that he created four more acts based on his grandmother's diary entries, merging her words with his memories and symbolism derived from U.S. and Japanese popular culture. A female voice is heard reading in English Toku's translated diary entries for each of the four new acts, while picture slides are shown of the corresponding act of the *Seven Kabuki Plays Project*. Viewers feel the power of Toku's words as Shimomura brings them visually to life. When a picture slide of the final act, act VII, "Montage," is projected, Shimomura explains another evolution from previous work, showing a picture slide of *Untitled*, his newest series of paintings that resembled this video art structure. Act VII is a summation of the six previous acts, presented in montage format, and is a watershed of imagery, memories, history, and symbolism from Shimomura's mind, thus reflecting another level of experimentation in his performance art as a nonlinear narrative.

The picture slides fade out and change to *Trans-Siberian Excerpts*. If the Katzmans are in the audience, Kurogo 1 makes a clacking noise, and Kurogo 2 comes to the podium to retrieve the book, titled *Little Red Train*, that Shimomura borrowed and return it to the Katzmans, with Shimomura thanking them and apologizing for keeping it for so long. Incorporating the audience into the performance art piece was also a new element that Shimomura would continue to modify and expand upon in his art; it enabled the artist to imprint his message, in what he referred to as a "subtextual" manner, meaning an off-stage and unscripted element of his performances, often with uncontrollable results. Here, the Katzmans are emblematic of this subtextual element. Shimomura cannot control whether they attend, and he has no control over their effect on the audience members to engage them in further understanding of the subtextual meaning they have on *Trans-Siberian Excerpts*.

A picture slide of a Polaroid photograph taken by Shimomura of a Soviet Pepsi bottle is shown. Shimomura explains that *Trans-Siberian Excerpts* is the first composed performance from a continuous and uninterrupted event, a seven-day journey across two continents, riding on the Trans-Siberian Railway. Shimomura describes that he brought 1960s post-bop jazz and Japanese rock and roll music on the seven-day journey and drafted twenty performance pieces inspired by the music and dramatic scenery that he viewed from his window, such as the Great Wall of China and the Siberian Desert. Shimomura was interested in issues of cultural mixing, cultural appropriation, cultural differences, cultural morality, and institutional power, before the existence of discourses on identity politics, multiculturalism, and cultural studies were established. As he continued his journey around the world, Shimomura explains that he revised his twenty pieces in Leningrad and London. Unfortunately, Shimomura states that he was robbed of all his materials upon his return to his hometown of Seattle, Washington. He immediately recreated eighteen of the twenty pieces, but his ancillary materials were gone. This photograph of a Soviet coke bottle that he had sent to his mother during his travels was the only evidence proving his trip; it symbolizes the global intersection of economies, branding, and U.S. pop culture encountered by Shimomura during his travels.

As Kurogo 2 gives away a *Trans-Siberian Excerpts* storyboard to a member of the audience, Shimomura elaborates briefly on the issues addressed in each of the nine pieces, which is accompanied by the following picture slides of each short piece: 1. Soviet Guards changing to Japanese male comic dancers; 2. "Set Me Free"; 3. Grandmother taking blood pressure and Grandma dead; 4. "Moon Seen as Exiles"; 5. "Junko's Song"; 6. "Playroom"; 7. "Minidoka Girls"; 8. "Hymn"; and 9. "Three Haiku." The performances referenced an array of subjects, such as Communist Russia, the suicide of Japanese women, Japanese American incarceration, Japanese pop music, Jayhawks football, potential causes of Toku's death, and Hawaiian Nisei veterans of World War II.

Picture slides change to photographs of students learning *Funky Odori* and video footage of the *Funky Odori* performance. Shimomura explains that he created *Funky Odori* for the Spring Festival at Eastern Illinois University, also in the vein of cultural transmission, mixing, and miscommunication. *Funky Odori* more closely resembled a happening[80] than his previous theater-based pieces. Shimomura videotaped the Bon Odori dance of Seattle Seafair's annual Obon Festival and asked Paludan to extrapolate movements she felt were of Japanese sensibility and to create a new "Japanese" dance that she taught to two students.

The audio of the *Funky Odori* music is played. Similarly, but composed separately, Shimomura describes giving Marty Olson, a local musician and artist, the tapes and samples of Japanese festival music to create his version of "Japanese" music—again, by extrapolating the Japanese essence of the sounds but funking up the beat. Shimomura's lecture explains that at the festival, Olson's music was played, and the two dancers whom Paludan had taught the *Funky Odori* encouraged students to learn the dance. The result was unlike anything Shimomura had ever seen, compared to the original Bon Odori he had filmed.

The audio changes to "Haiku Rap," an original composition by Tony Allard for *California Sushi*, and the picture slides change to photographs taken of *California Sushi*. Kurogo 1 gives away a storyboard of *California Sushi* to an audience member, and Shimomura begins to discuss this autobiographical collection of eight short performances and videos that examine the Asian American experience with a similar goal of cultivating further understanding and sensitivity to cultural differences.

A photograph of "Make Rice, Not War" appears. Shimomura explains that "Make Rice, Not War" bookmarks the opening and ending performances of *California Sushi*. A video clip shows Tony Allard, a performer, using militaristic movements to make rice using raw rice and plastic toy soldiers, all choreographed to "The Stars and Stripes Forever." Throughout the performance, the rice cooker cooks until it is done. *California Sushi* ends with Allard using similar militaristic movements to serve the rice-soldier concoction to the audience as they exit the theater in the hopes that they will chose peace, through understanding cultural differences, over war and discrimination. Shimomura not only references the life-altering impact of World War II and his Japanese cultural roots but also his military service as a U.S. citizen.

Then Shimomura shows a video clip of each act in *California Sushi*. As the audience sees the video clip of "Valeda Daze", referring to a Japanese American sorority, Shimomura enumerates that "Valeda Daze" comments on a white-only clause in the Greek system at the University of Washington, his undergraduate university, through the 1960s, that forced ethnic groups to organize segregated sororities and fraternities. Shimomura explains his participation in the piece as an eighteen-year-old freshman dancing the cha-cha and a fifty-year-old man attempting to relive his youth, although in his elder years, he dances out of beat and to the wrong music. Shimomura emphasizes the racial tensions by adding an Asian American girl who prefers to dance with a life-sized inflatable Superman doll that she emasculates by pulling out his plug. Superman is symbolic of an idyllic U.S., white, male society that is clearly not a "real" dance partner. Then Shimomura shows a video of Professor Doty, a fellow faculty member who danced in protest of his performance piece, arguing her affection for Superman and not understanding the meaning of Shimomura's symbolism.

The video changes to the third piece, "K.I.K.E." (meaning "kinky, immature, kimono, empress"), which came from a casual conversation with a Jewish acquaintance. Shimomura explains that he was asked if he knew what a J.A.P. ("Jewish American princess") was, with no recognition or disclaimer of the origins of the acronym and why it carries familiarity in U.S. culture. "K.I.K.E." is a word play that Shimomura created to reference the use of a historic derogatory term in a joking and culturally unrelated manner. Shimomura performed this piece at his first opening at the Bernice Steinbaum Gallery and received telling emotional responses by several Jewish audience members, demonstrating that the parallels between the racial slurs *jap* and *kike* were clearly communicated, and Shimomura was successful in transmitting greater awareness of cultural histories and sensitivity of cultural differences.

The audience sees a video clip of "Tai-Pan Cappy." "Tai-Pan Cappy" refers to a different type of cultural insensitivity, as a Western professor of Japanese history and long-time resident of Japan (over half his twenty-year career) is interviewed as a cultural authority figure of Japan. As the title references, Tai-Pan Cappy is a cultural tourist, and the professor lacks any true awareness of Japanese culture. The interviewer's increasing frustration is evident with each answered question that is asked in an attempt to learn about Japanese culture.

As a video clip of "He" is shown, Shimomura explains that this was his most direct, autobiographical performance describing recurring symbolism in Shimomura's art, such as blond hair, patent leather shoes, gloves, hammer, airplanes, a Mickey Mouse doll, and a gun. These objects were presented with an accompanying journal entry to describe an event in Shimomura's life, similar to the way his grandmother's journals operate with his paintings and performance art. Shimomura draws on his personal experiences as a Sansei to construct the jarring cultural mixings and racial encounters that take place in Asian American life. As an autobiographical endeavor, this was yet another step in his performance art, exploring situations that created emotional imprints in Shimomura's memory.

As the video clip of "Better Homes" is played, Shimomura describes the misperception that Japanese Americans willingly accepted the injustice of their incarceration, and his discovery of anonymous poems expressing internees' discontent among his grandmother's writings proves that Japanese Americans did not willingly accept the actions of the U.S. government. The video changes to a clip of "Yellow No (All) Same." "Yellow No (All) Same" used video and picture slide comparisons of Japanese and Chinese culture, such as Kabuki theater and Chinese Opera, pointing out the differences with text that stated "Kabuki is not Chinese." The inverse concept "Yellow All Same" was borrowed from Lawson Inada's poem that addressed how Chinese Americans capitalized on the incarceration of Japanese Americans and the closure of Japanese restaurants, reopening the restaurant under Chinese American ownership and stating they were offering "essentially" the same "yellow" cuisine. A kurogo hands out "Yellow No (All) Same" buttons to audience members. Also, the phrase "yellow all the same" refers to a negative perception that all Asians look and act alike with no acknowledgment or awareness of their vastly different cultures and histories. The only positive aspect of pan-Asian solidarity, which does not promote the stereotype of "yellow all the same," was rooted in the ethnic studies movement to gain larger political presence and social justice through an Asian American identity.

Four picture slides of the making of *The Last Sansei Story* are shown, and a kurogo gives away a storyboard of *The Last Sansei Story* to a member of the audience. Shimomura, continuing his lecture/performance, describes *The Last Sansei Story* as an homage to the three generations of Japanese Americans. Shimomura states that this was the largest undertaking in his performance art career, with a cast and crew of twenty-one people and a twelve-venue touring schedule. Shimomura explains that the piece was based on the artist hearing his youngest daughter speak Japanese after one year of study. Her English accent was prominent because she had no exposure to hearing a native speaker, such as her Issei great-grandmother, and this led him to believe the Japanese American experience was over because no direct connection to Japan was available.

As picture slides of "Prelude" and act one, "The Issei" are shown, Shimomura recreates the audience participation component of *The Last Sansei Story* by having kurogos dart around the auditorium giving communion and handing out photo cards of babies Toku delivered to create subtextual moments through his performance art. "Prelude" discusses Toku Shimomura's life in Japan as a Red Cross nurse during the Russo-Japanese War, and act one, "The Issei," documents her immigration to the United States as a picture bride; passing the state of Washington's midwife exam; and her career, delivering over one thousand babies in the United States.

Next, posters of *Campfire Diary*,[81] the solo version of act two, "The Nisei," are handed out to the audience by kurogos, while Shimomura describes how the rewrite of the *Seven Kabuki Plays Project* took its final form. Picture slides of *Campfire Diary* are shown as Shimomura explains that the foundation for *Campfire Diary* came from his grandmother's journal entries from the attack on Pearl Harbor to Christmas incarcerated at Minidoka, in Hunt, Idaho, but the arrangement departs from the moments surrounding his paintings to reflect Shimomura's mature performance-art style.

The picture slides change to show act three, "The Sansei," which addresses topics from Shimomura's own life such as the model minority myth, stereotypes of Asians in U.S. popular culture (specifically referencing television and movies), segregation in U.S. universities, Japan-bashing in U.S. media through the return of the "yellow peril" stereotypes, and intolerance promoted through Christian evangelicals like Tammy Faye Bakker. While fragments of Japanese culture exist in Shimomura's life, they are heavily filtered through U.S. society's myriad voices, and very few of these representations reflect positive, direct connections to Japan.

Picture slides of *Yellow Potluck*, an installation, and Kwang Yu Fong and her performance, *Fortune Cookies Are Not Japanese*, are displayed. Although the connection to Japan and its Issei immigrants to the United States was severed, this neither accounts for the postwar and contemporary Japanese immigrants nor the mixed-race Japanese Americans, and Shimomura aptly tackles these topics in *Yellow Potluck/Fortune Cookies Are Not Japanese*. Ironically, this performance was particularly enjoyable for Shimomura because Kwang Yu Fong answered his advertisement for a contemporary performance artist with a background in Chinese opera in less than three hours, demonstrating the globalized and cosmopolitan nature of places like New York City. In this multicultural piece, Kwang danced to Chinese opera music, wore Chinese opera makeup, and dressed in Western attire, while handing out fortune cookies that read "Fortune cookies are not Japanese." Kwang pointed out that fortune cookies were not Chinese either, articulating that generalizations and stereotypes destroy opportunities to garner a cultural sensitivity to difference.

A picture slide of Kelley Hunt, singer and performer, with a kurogo from *Songs for a Rickshaw Boy* is shown. Simultaneously, Hunt enters the lecture hall of *A Decade of Performances*, dressed similarly to her appearance in the picture slide, and sings one of her four songs. She is followed by a kurogo holding a grocery bag full of Wonder Bread, potatoes, cakes, apple pie, vanilla ice cream, wieners, hotdog buns, Campbell's ramen, teriyaki mix, Campbell's wonton soup, apples, catsup, and other items that symbolize, through material culture—specifically here as food—the awkwardness of acculturation.

Shimomura describes how *Songs for a Rickshaw Boy* demonstrates the difficulties of acculturating to Japan or the United States. *Songs for a Rickshaw Boy* was performed less than a month before *A Decade of Performance Art... Not Made in Japan* as part of Shimomura's twenty-five year retrospective in Seattle, Washington. Audience members experience a sense of the superficial nature of these objects and brands, and yet understand the strength of their meaning as part of U.S. cultural identity. The performance ends after Hunt completes her song, and the kurogo passes out the final groceries. Shimomura's *A Decade of Performances* boldly creates and dissects U.S. pop culture through the lens of the Japanese American experience.

Keiko Kira as Nisei (Photograph by Roger Shimomura, *December Haiku*, September 20, 1996, Bellevue Arts Museum: Bellevue, Washington).

december haiku

- **Bellevue Arts Museum, Bellevue, Washington, September 20, 1996**

December Haiku is a two-hour performance piece that consists of a single performer in front of the "Nisei Wall" installation, which resembles the barracks wall shared by the Shimomura family at the Minidoka incarceration center during Christmas. Shimomura reworks the *Three Haikus* piece from *Trans-Siberian Excerpts* using the same three haikus written by Toku Shimomura. However, in *December Haiku*, Shimomura has consolidated the three haikus into three symbolic objects and an electronic message board displaying them in romanized kanji that sits underneath the Christmas tree (which literally is a branch from a tumbleweed). Furthermore, the warrior is now a female, and her movements are imperceptible to the human eye. The performance begins when she suddenly appears through the ten-foot-wide opening in the "Nisei Wall," dressed in a kimono and a head and mouth scarf, and with her face painted. The performer moves imperceptibly slowly, from right to left, in front of the "Nisei Wall" over the next two hours, dropping three objects along the way: a small wooden cross, an origami bird made from Walt Disney wrapping paper, and a children's wooden block with the image of a cat and the word 'cat' written in Japanese. The music alters every thirty minutes between slow droning chords and dissonant versions of Christmas carols. Shimomura uses a warrior to connote the wartime atmosphere when his grandmother wrote the haikus. The warrior gains an upper hand through the use of patience, quiet, and the unseen. These are perhaps qualities of the Japanese American experience, and they are very different from the visible power and force reflective of American values.

In this performance, the three objects represent the three haikus:

The Cross
This is the place where
I bury my son
who died in the war.

The Crane
For twenty years I
Raised him to make him an
enemy of my country.

The Wooden Block
Drafted by our enemy
My son learned
the Japanese language.

Shimomura has altered the symbolism to reflect more closely the context of the time and place that Toku wrote these three haikus. The first haiku refers to any son in any war and mourning the loss of a child as the most devastating life experience. The second haiku refers to children. Toku brought over one thousand children into the world as a midwife. The effects of war on children are another devastatingly traumatic aspect of war and part of Shimomura's personal experience. Using the example of a Japanese American family, Issei immigrants were now enemies to their Japanese relatives; Japanese American citizens were considered enemies of the United States; and Nisei soldiers, who were imprisoned as enemies of the United States, were permitted to fight on behalf of the United States to prove their loyalty as U.S. citizens. The third haiku is another paradox of the Japanese American experience, as the "enemy" refers to the United States drafting of Nisei into the U.S. military and teaching the Nisei son to speak his ethnic "enemy" language to aid in counter intelligence. Yet, post-Pearl Harbor, being in possession of objects with Japanese writing was grounds for imprisonment and was viewed as treason. All three scenarios were traumatic and were experienced by Japanese Americans during World War II: American citizens who became the "enemy" because of Japanese ancestry in their U.S. home, relatives in Japan who were seen as "enemy," and drafted Nisei sons who were permitted to learn about their "enemy" ancestry once unjustly imprisoned.

Poly Reyes as Toku (Photograph by Roger Shimomura, *La Carta*, October 11, 2001, Lied Center of Kansas, University of Kansas: Lawrence, Kansas).

la carta

12

- **Lied Center of Kansas, University of Kansas, Lawrence, Kansas, October 11, 2001**

Shimomura explores a new performance sensibility in his last two performance pieces, *La Carta* and *Amnesia*. Whereas before, the artist provides copious amounts of imagery, layers of media, and decades of history in his pieces, in *La Carta* he now distills his vast collections of popular-culture songs, films, television shows, toys, comic books, and stereotypical imagery into a singular and focused format. *La Carta* is an homage to his grandmother's life and accomplishments in the United States for fifty-six years. A solo female flamenco dancer performs two dances encapsulating Toku's life in the United States, punctuated by World War II.

The theater is dark, and music of Tibetan chanting is heard, followed by accelerating gong sounds, as a large Chinese parasol is lowered from the ceiling, stopping ten feet above the stage. The umbrella is a symbol connecting heaven (the sky) and earth (the staff), and it evokes Toku Shimomura (1888–1968) returning to read her letter that describes her life and accomplishments in the United States. It was very customary for Issei to reach out to relatives in this manner. The Tibetan chanting similarly evokes communicating with ancestors and gods. A female voice begins to read Toku's letter as it was written in Japanese as a large video projection of a hand writing the last letter appears in the background. Suddenly, a flamenco dancer rushes onto the stage and begins dancing to the chanting, an atypical musical score for flamenco but a likely combination and one that is symbolic of divergent cultural juxtapositions in Shimomura's mind. Halfway through the dance, a blue light illuminates a pile of babies, symbolizing the one-thousand-plus lives Toku brought into the world as a Japanese American midwife for twenty-five years. Shimomura uses colored spotlights as lenses—blue meaning memory and evoking the past, and yellow as racist.

The video, along with the female voice reading the letter and the chanting, fade away, and a second spotlight illuminates a different area of the stage. As the *compas*[82], traditional flamenco music, begins, the flamenco dancer lets her hair down and starts her second dance [IMAGE 163]. A kurogo hands her a red shawl, symbolizing World War II. The video projection of a hand writing the letter in Japanese resumes, and halfway through the second dance, the kurogo reappears, pushing a guard tower across the stage in front of the screen, symbolizing the Japanese American incarceration. In total, the two dances last approximately ten minutes, corresponding to the length of Toku's letter to her relatives.

Although *La Carta*, translates to "The Letter" in Spanish and relies little on U.S. pop culture, it very much highlights cultural awareness of differences through the mixing of dance, video, theater, and music in trademark Shimomura fashion. The Japanese American experience is presented through an international lens, with complex rhythms and bold, elegant movements. Interestingly, flamenco originated in Spain but grew internationally in popularity. Now the highest concentration of flamenco dance academies resides in the United States and Japan. Shimomura was perhaps also referencing the global experience of Japanese Americans with the largest concentration of Asian immigrants in South America, predominantly Brazil.

IMAGE 163: Detail (Photograph by Roger Shimomura, *La Carta*, October 11, 2001, Lied Center of Kansas, University of Kansas: Lawrence, Kansas).

Keiko Kira as Toku (Photograph by Roger Shimomura, *Amnesia*, January 10-11, 2002, Bellevue Arts Museum: Bellevue, Washington).

13

amnesia

- **Bellevue Arts Museum, Auditorium, Bellevue, Washington, January 10–11, 2002**

As the title describes, *Amnesia* is about the complexities surrounding the issue of forgetting past experiences of Asian Americans, specifically their racial and discriminatory history in the United States that began at the time of their immigration during the 1850s. Juxtaposed with the contemporary and shifting sociopolitical landscape between the United States and Asian countries since the Cold War era, and the ever-increasing fluidity of travel and international communication, Shimomura creates *Amnesia* to address attitudes held by contemporary diasporic Asians and Asian Americans, who feel no connection to the past negative treatment of Asians and who generally believe these issues to be over and irrelevant to their identity. Simultaneously, U.S. popular culture remains enthusiastic for operas and musicals, such as *Madame Butterfly* and *Miss Saigon*, that offer stereotypical representations of Asians through a colonial lens, demonstrating that attitudes from a century ago are still in existence. Shimomura finds such favoritism for negative depictions of Asians symbolic of deep-rooted stereotypical and divisive attitudes still present in U.S. society. More troubling, such attitudes have enabled violent and unlawful actions against people of Asian heritage, resulting in minimal to no legal ramifications. The continued presence and promotion of such negative depictions of persons of Asian heritage is precisely why Shimomura's work, and the work of artists like Renee Tajima-Peña, exists.

The Prelude opens with a low-volume audio track from *Crouching Tiger, Hidden Dragon* while the audience is seated. On the dimly lit stage sits a female performer with her back to the audience. She wears a red evening gown and blood pressure cuff. She is bent over, peering at a television that can be seen between a small crack formed by two shoji [IMAGE 165]. Once the audience is seated, the audio track increases in volume so that it is audible by the audience for one minute. The performer begins to move her body to get a better angle of the television through the narrow opening. The soundtrack fades out as the sound of a heartbeat begins. Kurogo 1 uncovers

IMAGE 165: Detail (Photograph by Roger Shimomura, *Amnesia*, January 10-11, 2002, Bellevue Arts Museum: Bellevue, Washington).

the electronic message board displaying blood pressure readings, and the performer stands up, spotlit by Kurogo 2, and faces the audience while taking her blood pressure. Staring at the gauge, she sighs in despair and is unilluminated by Kurogo 2, while Kurogo 1 covers the message board displaying the blood pressure readings. The performer picks up her chair and exits the stage, while Kurogos 1 and 2 remove the television, message board, and shoji from the stage.

The performer represents Toku Shimomura, Roger's grandmother, a nurse and midwife, who recorded her blood pressure due to hypertension likely caused by traumatic events in her life, such as World War II and her subsequent incarceration. Toku is symbolic of the history of Asian Americans that is arguably irrelevant to the contemporary Asian culture represented by *Crouching Tiger, Hidden Dragon*, the highest-grossing foreign language film in American history, winning three Academy Awards, including Best Picture. Shimomura selects this Chinese film to reflect his "Yellow No (All) Same" performance that attempts to educate viewers about the difference between Japanese and Chinese culture to disempower attitudes and stereotypes that remove major cultural differences among Asians, viewing them as all the same. This film differs from stereotypical portrayals of Asians because it is directed by Ang Lee, has an international cast, and was produced outside the United States. The landmark success of this Asian martial arts love story is a significant benchmark, but Shimomura does not grant Toku or the audience complete access to the film because its success is not reflective of the current state of Asian American visual representation in the United States. The shoji accentuate the differences between Japanese and Chinese culture, symbolically dividing past and present attitudes of Asian immigrants and Asian Americans in the United States.

The Move

Act I, "The Move," opens with the fading of the heartbeat sound as a yellow spotlight illuminates one of two kotos. Elizabeth Falconer, an internationally recognized koto player, composer, and recording artist, enters the stage wearing a brightly colored kimono and cowboy hat [IMAGE 166]. The brief sound of a railroad crossing is heard before Falconer plays "Don't Fence Me In," a pop tune, on the bass koto. Shimomura is referencing the forced incarceration of Japanese Americans during World War II to incarceration

IMAGE 166: Elizabeth Falconer (Photograph by Roger Shimomura, *Amnesia*, January 10-11, 2002, Bellevue Arts Museum: Bellevue, Washington).

centers at remote locations in the Midwest. The Shimomura family, along with approximately twelve thousand other Japanese Americans, was relocated to Minidoka, in Hunt, Idaho. The song is from the 1944 musical film, *Hollywood Canteen*, about two Caucasian American soldiers on leave for three days from World War II before returning to fight in the South Pacific. It was the fourth highest grossing film of the year and received three Academy Award nominations, winning one award for best original song. Shimomura selected this song as a historical snapshot of not only the subject matter but also of U.S. attitudes of this period. When applied to the Japanese American experience simultaneously taking place, the irony of the song's title, "Don't Fence Me In," and the lyrics promoting American ideals of freedom are part of Shimomura's dark humor. Using the koto instead of a guitar further emphasizes the lack of musical (and visual, referring to the film) presence of Asian Americans in U.S. popular culture.

As Falconer finishes the song the yellow spotlight fades to black and the audience hears the sound of a train approaching to a video projection of train tracks. Falconer removes her kimono and cowgirl hat to reveal black clothes, and she moves to sit behind the second bass koto as Kurogo 2 takes her clothing items off stage, and Kurogo 1 removes the cloth covering the suitcases. As the train sound fades, a blue light illuminates Falconer and the stage as she begins to play "Moon and Stars." Thirty seconds into the song, Toku enters the stage for her solo. She wears everyday 1940s attire and carries a washboard [IMAGE 167]. Toku opens her one suitcase permitted for her incarceration and holds up Japanese characters and Roman numerals that symbolize her forced move to Minidoka. Once the seven-minutes-and-ten-second song is over, the blue light is turned off. Falconer exits the stage, taking one suitcase, followed by Toku who takes one suitcase, and the kurogos who take all remaining suitcases. They are accompanied by sounds of the native inhabitants of the land; coyote howls and rattlesnake shakers are symbolic of the desert wilderness and were new dangers the Japanese Americans faced every night.

As these sounds fade out, Kari Paludan, a soprano and an opera and theater performer and teacher, enters, dressed in elegant 1940s attire including an evening gown and a large brimmed hat, and she operatically sings "Don't Fence Me In." [IMAGE 168] Once she begins her solo, a picture slideshow video of the Japanese American incarceration is shown. The song ends in unison with the video, and the audience hears rattlesnakes again. Paludan

Top, IMAGE 167: Detail.

Bottom, IMAGE 168: Kari Paludan.

(Photographs by Roger Shimomura, *Amnesia*, January 10-11, 2002, Bellevue Arts Museum: Bellevue, Washington).

becomes the Japanese American protagonist in Shimomura's version of the *Hollywood Canteen*, by inserting the Japanese American experience and recoding the meaning of "Don't Fence Me In."

The Internment

Kurogo 2 moves the blue spotlight to the back of the theater and awaits Toku's entrance. Act II, "The Internment," begins with a bugle sounding a reveille, a typical wake-up call for U.S. military personnel. The context is not a military base, but instead, Minidoka, as a barbed-wire picture slide is projected. Off stage, Paludan begins singing "Depuis le Jour," a cappella, as Toku, dressed in work clothes and headscarf, and carrying a wash basin, enters through the back of the theater, lit by Kurogo 2. Upon reaching the stage, she pins clothes to a clothesline, using slow, methodical, repetitious movements, for four minutes until the song is over [IMAGE 169]. "Depuis le Jour" is the most famous aria from *Louise*, a turn-of-the-century opera about a Parisian working-class seamstress who yearns for freedom offered by the modern city of Paris; it was selected by Shimomura to parallel the story of French women's struggles in French society with Japanese American women's struggles in American society—although, again, the artist recodes the female protagonist as Toku doing the wash at Minidoka while yearning for freedom from her unjust imprisonment. Watching Toku repetitiously pin clothes for only four minutes provides a small insight into the monotonous existence of incarceration, not to mention laundry and other forms of "women's work."

Loss of Memory

Act III, "Loss of Memory," features a documentary video by Renee Tajima-Peña, titled *Skate Manzanar*, that is approximately six minutes in length. Shimomura wrote a script that he discussed with Tajima-Peña, who then shot the film. This was the first time *Skate Manzanar* was shown. The documentary captures a Japanese American teenager skateboarding the ruins of Manzanar, one of ten incarceration centers—a remote, desolate, desert terrain full of rocks, scrub bushes, and obviously not an ideal place for skating [IMAGE 170]. Although few structures remain, an obelisk with kanji demarking the cemetery is the clearest reference to the horrific history of the Japanese American internees. Six confirmed bodies remain buried at the site: three bachelors with no known family to claim their bodies and three babies. The title of the act, "Loss of Memory" is exactly what is explored, as

IMAGE 169: Keiko Kira as Toku (Photograph by Roger Shimomura, *Amnesia*, January 10-11, 2002, Bellevue Arts Museum: Bellevue, Washington).

Top, IMAGE 170: *Skate Manzanar*, Directed by Renee Tajima-Peña, 2001, video still (Photograph by Roger Shimomura, *Amnesia*, January 10-11, 2002, Bellevue Arts Museum: Bellevue, Washington).

Bottom, IMAGE 171: Keiko Kira as Karaoke Singer (Photograph by Roger Shimomura, *Amnesia*, January 10-11, 2002, Bellevue Arts Museum: Bellevue, Washington).

viewers question why a teenager would travel to Death Valley, a remote and harsh environment, to skate ruins. Tajima-Peña uses the skater's perspective to move sideways (as opposed to forward) through the space to symbolically give a new perspective to Manzanar. Manzanar appears as a forgotten landscape, and yet the very act of skating—a contemporary activity—and being present reclaims the loss, at least partially, and brings new life to the site. Although the skater would never have access to the lived experience of internees, he chose to skate Manzanar and be among his ancestors.

Lost Memory

Act IV, "Lost Memory," differs from the prior act as the action of losing is now complete—there is no memory of the Japanese American incarceration. "Ladies' Night" by Kool and the Gang opens the act, along with a disco ball. A female Asian performer, dressed in 1980s clothes and a blond curly wig, and Paludan, dressed similarly but without a wig, are seated side by side and dance in their chairs to the music for the first minute and a half of the song. The celebration continues while the dance music fades out, and the audience sees a video of *The Little Shop of Horrors* with no sound. The song of Momoe (Yamaguchi Momoe), "Yokosuka Sutori," begins, and the contemporary Asian female lip-synchs the first part of the song, giving a Japanese female singer impression on a Mr. Microphone [IMAGE 171]. Then she hands the microphone to Paludan before exiting stage. For the last forty seconds of the song, Paludan stands and sings live in perfect Japanese to the orchestral background of the song.

Shimomura gives Paludan, the Japanese American protagonist, a voice, while the contemporary Asian female is only permitted mimicry. The hollow impersonation by the Asian female is superficial, and while the music is celebratory, there is an emptiness and disconnect to the prior acts, as no reference to Japanese American culture or history is provided. A heartbeat sound is heard one final time before everything fades to black to remind the audience of the temporal nature of human life and cultural memory.

Epilogue

Act V, "Epilogue," is Shimomura's response to the lost memory of the Japanese American experience and, more broadly, Asian American history. Paludan, dressed in *Madame Butterfly* kimono and wearing Asian eye makeup, enters to the heartbeat sounds and begins singing "Un Bel di Vedremo,"

IMAGE 172: Kari Paludan (Photograph by Roger Shimomura, *Amnesia*, January 10-11, 2002, Bellevue Arts Museum: Bellevue, Washington).

the most famous aria from *Madame Butterfly*, to a recorded orchestra [IMAGE 172]. After completing the song, Paludan exits, and the nocturnal sounds of incarceration arise; wind, coyotes, and rattlesnakes haunt the darkness and stillness. A projection of the guard towers is shown, and a monk with a basket over her head walks aimlessly across the projection, using a shovel as a walking stick [IMAGE 173]. Upon exiting the stage, the Japanese words for *hot*, *cold*, *windy*, *dusty*, and *crowded* are heard over the sound of wind, which increases in volume and intensity. The audience hears the word *shigatakanai* (meaning "it cannot be helped"), and the wind sounds again, blowing away the memory. Shimomura repeats this again, "*shikata ga nai*," louder, and more wind crescendoes—until finally, there is silence.

The history and memory of the Japanese American experience is relegated to the wind to pass along to the audience. Shimomura cannot forget the history of Asian Americans while stereotypical portrayals of Asian Americans exist and continue to be shown in popular culture through operas and musicals like *Madame Butterfly* and *Miss Saigon*, which glorify Asian women's obeisance to American military men, through suicide and forfeiting their multiracial children. Shimomura finds such portrayals highly offensive and detrimental to equality and the understanding of cultural differences, especially after personally experiencing incarceration as a three-year-old

IMAGE 173: Keiko Kira as Monk (Photograph by Roger Shimomura, *Amnesia*, January 10-11, 2002, Bellevue Arts Museum: Bellevue, Washington).

toddler for no reason other than being of Japanese ancestry. "Amnesia," and all of Shimomura's performance art (including his entire oeuvre), counter stereotypical portrayals of Asian Americans, promote awareness of cultural differences, and garner greater sensitivity and respect of others. Shimomura creates his own artistic language (whether painting, performance, music, costume, or set design) using popular culture and reflecting broadly held cultural values and historically significant artifacts that range from his family's personal history to Japanese and American material culture to express the complexities and nuances of the Japanese American experience.

Selected Bibliography

Baudrillard, Jean. *The Consumer Society: Myths and Structures*. London: Sage, 1998.

Bhabha, Homi K. *Location of Culture*. New York: Routledge, 1994.

Butler, Judith. *Gender Trouble: Feminism and the Subversion of Identity*. New York: Routledge, 1990.

Chan, Sucheng. *Asian Americans: An Interpretative History*. Boston: Twayne, 1991.

Chang, Alexandra. *Envisioning Diaspora: Asian American Visual Art Collectives from Godzilla Godzookie to the Barnstormers*. Beijing: Timezone 8 Editions, 2008.

Chang, Gordon, Paul Karlstrom, and Mark Dean Johnson. *Asian American Art: A History 1850–1970*. Palo Alto: Stanford University Press, 2008.

Cheng, Anne. *The Melancholy of Race: Psychoanalysis, Assimilation, and Hidden Grief*. New York: Oxford University Press, 2001.

Chiu, Melissa, Karin Higa, and Susette S. Min. *One Way or Another: Asian American Art Now*. New Haven: Yale University Press and Asia Society, 2006.

Daniels, Roger. *Prisoners without Trial: Japanese Americans in World War II*. New York: Hill and Wang, 1993.

Debord, Guy. *Society of the Spectacle*. Translated by Ken Knabb. London: Rebel Press, 1967.

Eaton, Allen H. *Beauty Behind Barbed Wire: The Arts of the Japanese in Our War Relocation Camps*. New York: Harper and Brothers Publishers, 1952.

Fanon, Franz. *Black Skin/White Masks*. Translated by Richard Philcox. New York: Grove Press, 1967.

Foucault, Michel. *Discipline and Punish: The Birth of the Prison*. Translated by Alan Sheridan. New York: Vintage Books, 1977.

Hall, Stuart. *Representation, Vol. 2: Cultural Representations and Signifying Practices*. London: Sage, 1997.

Higa, Karin. *A View from Within: Japanese American Art from the Internment Camps, 1942–1945*. Los Angeles: Japanese American National Museum, UCLA Wright Art Gallery and UCLA Asian American Studies Center, 1992.

Hirasuna, Delphine. *The Art of Gaman: Arts and Crafts from the Japanese American Internment Camps, 1942–1946*. Berkeley: Ten Speed Press, 2005.

Hosokawa, Bill. *Nisei: The Quiet Americans*. New York: William Morrow and Company Inc., 1969.

Kim, Claire Jean. “The Racial Triangulation of Asian Americans.” *Politics & Society* 27, no.1 (March 1999): 105–138.

Kim, Elaine, Margo Machida, and Sharon Mizota. *Fresh Talk/ Daring Gazes: Conversations on Asian American Art*. Los Angeles: University of California Press, 2003.

Lee, Anthony. *Picturing Chinatown: Art and Orientalism in San Francisco*. Los Angeles: University of California Press, 2001.

Lee, Josephine, Imogene L. Lim, and Yuko Matsukawa. *Re/collecting Early Asian America: Essay in Cultural History*. Philadelphia: Temple University Press, 2002.

Lippard, Lucy. *Mixed Blessings*. New York: The New Press, 1990.

Machida, Margo, Vishakha N. Desai, and John Kuo Wei Tchen. *Asia/America: Identities in Contemporary Asian American Art*. New York: The Asia Society Galleries and the New Press, 1994.

Machida, Margo. *Unsettled Vision: Contemporary Asian American Artists and the Social Imaginary.* Durham: Duke University Press, 2008.

Mimura, Glen M. *Ghostlife of Third Cinema: Asian American Film and Video*. Minneapolis: University of Minnesota Press, 2009.

Okihiro, Gary Y. “Japanese Resistance in America’s Concentration Camps: A Reevaluation.” *Amerasia Journal* 2, no. 1 (Fall 1973), 20–34.

Pegler-Gordon, Anna. “Chinese Exclusion, Photography, and the Development of U.S. Immigration Policy.” *American Quarterly* 58, no. 1 (2006): 51–77.

Reed, Dennis. *Japanese Photography in America, 1920–1940*. Los Angeles: Japanese American Cultural and Community Center and Doizaki Gallery, 1985.

Said, Edward W. *The World, the Text, and the Critic*. Cambridge: Harvard University Press, 1983.

Wang, ShiPu. *Becoming American? The Art and Identity of Yasuo Kuniyoshi.* Honolulu: University of Hawai'i Press, 2011.

Wechsler, Jeffrey. *Asian Traditions/ Modern Expressions: Asian American Artists and Abstraction.* New York: Harry N. Abrams and Jane Voorhees Zimmerli Art Museum, 1997.

Weglyn, Michi. *Years of Infamy: The Untold Story of America's Concentration Camps*. New York: William Morrow and Company Inc., 1976.

Winther-Tamaki, Bert. *Art in the Encounter of Nations*. Honolulu: University of Hawai'i Press, 2001.

Yang, Alice. *Why Asia? Contemporary Asian and Asian American Art*. New York: New York University Press, 1998.

Yoshimoto, Midori. *Into Performance: Japanese Women Artists in New York*. New Brunswick: Rutgers University Press, 2005.

End Notes

1 Filmmaking has been of interest to Shimomura since his graduate studies. Shimomura studied filmmaking while at Syracuse University and considered changing his major after completing his first and only film. Later, the artist almost accepted a university position in Wisconsin as the filmmaker of a "happening" tour group, but he was ultimately more impressed with the University of Kansas's painting department and accepted that faculty job.

2 A kurogo is a stage assistant in Japanese theater who dresses in all black and facilitates the play through actions such as moving props and expediting costume changes. Although kurogos are visible and integral to the performance, they are not meant to affect the narrative of the performance.

3 Experimental theater opposes bourgeois theater by challenging its hierarchical structure but takes theater (as opposed to other art forms) as its sole discipline of analysis.

4 The "Other" operates as a postcolonial term in Shimomura works, both in a social and psychological sense, through a colonist lens of colonizer and colonized, in which one group excludes or marginalizes another group. In tandem with Orientalism, the process where European studies and culture constructed "the Orient," during the eighteenth century, as an exotic Other through broad generalizations about Islamic and Asian cultures, the Other represents that which was opposite or dissimilar to western thinking, especially in stereotypical images.

5 "The Gaze" is a postcolonial term that is also referred to as the "postcolonial gaze," as well as "orientalism" according to Edward Said's book titled *Orientalism*. The Gaze exposes the subject/object, or colonizer/colonized relationship, specifically the colonizer's understanding of self is based directly in contrast to how it views and positions the colonized, as Other. Because the postcolonial gaze recognizes and identifies the construction of the Other, it can be dismantled and overcome.

6 Ukiyo-e is defined as "pictures of the floating world" primarily made through woodblock printing. Ukiyo-e was popular during and reflective of the Edo period, seventeenth through nineteenth centuries. Because ukiyo-e subject matter included geishas, courtesans, kabuki actors, and scenes from folk tales, reflective of the rising merchant classes' interests in entertainment, ukiyo-e is a well-suited signifier of fantasy, further validating its fetishized quality and signification in Shimomura's art.

7 Roger Shimomura, Interview with the artist, February 4, 2017.

8 Coterminous with the artist's eighteen-year period of performance art, Shimomura created several series of paintings, such as "Diary," "Montage (Untitled)," "Return of the Yellow

Peril," "American Diary," "Jap's a Jap," and "Stereotypes and Admonitions."

9 Kabuki is a popular form of Japanese theater that emerged during the Edo period, 1603–1868.

10 Issei is a term that describes the first generation of Japanese immigrants to the United States.

11 Jonathan Flatley, "Warhol Gives Good Face: Publicity and the Politics of Prosopopoeia," in *Pop Out: Queer Warhol* (eds. Jennifer Doyle, Jonathan Flatley, and José Esteban Muñoz, Duke University Press, 1996), 100.

12 Ibid, 104.

13 Ibid, 104.

14 Ibid, 105.

15 Roger Shimomura, Interview with the artist, September 26, 2016. More information on this project can be accessed on the Creative Time website <http://creativetime.org/projects/42nd-street-art-project-2/>.

16 Shimomura's performances fall into the realm of both performance art and experimental theater.

17 The death of Toku, Shimomura's grandmother, was attributed to high blood pressure and heart failure.

18 Brunson music is a blend of several musical influences, such as 1980s rhythm and blues, electro-funk, and break dance.

19 Roger Shimomura, *A Decade of Performance Art...Not Made in Japan*, Production Script, 3–4.

20 Incarceration refers to the legally permissible detention of persons deemed enemy aliens—non-U.S. citizens—during war by the army or the Department of Justice. Incarceration is thought to be a more accurate term, referring to two-thirds of the Japanese American population, who were U.S. citizens.

21 Roger Shimomura, The *Seven Kabuki Plays Project*, Production Script, 1984.

22 Roger Shimomura, Interview with the author, May 14, 2016.

23 Toku was Issei and not eligible for citizenship until 1952. But two-thirds of Japanese Americans imprisoned were U.S. citizens by birth, including Roger, who was three years old at the time of incarceration.

24 Shimomura, The *Seven Kabuki Plays Project*, Production Script, 1984.

25 For more information on this topic, please refer to *Rohwer* by Lionelle Hamanaka, *Behind Enemy Lines* by Rosanna Yamagiwa Alfaro, and *Station J* by Richard France. (<http://www.nytimes.com/1982/03/12/theater/3-dramas-on-japanese-american-internment-days.html>).

26 For more information on Kabuki, please refer to *Staging Japanese Theater: Noh and Kabuki* (1994) by John Mitchell and Miyoko Watanabe, and *Creating Kabuki* (2010) by Katherine Saltzman-Li.

27 Shimomura was given this book by David Katzman and referred to it as *Little Red Train* in *A Decade of Performance Art...Not Made in Japan*, Production Script, 7.

28 Also stolen were Shimomura's two checkbooks; $2,000 in cash; his favorite ring; a Polaroid camera; a 35 mm Nikon camera; and two portable tape recorders. Shimomura, Interview with the artist, May 14, 2016.

29 Kibei Nisei refers to the 1.5 generation Japanese Americans. The Kibei Nisei were born in the United States and were American citizens, but returned to Japan to be educated through Japanese schooling before returning to the United State in pursuit of a college degree or occupation. They were often discriminated again by their Nisei peers as being too Japanese.

30 Roger Shimomura, *Trans-Siberian Excerpts,* Production Script, 1987.

31 Ibid.

32 Authorship of this poem is unknown. It came from Toku's translated materials of her Issei haiku club while she was incarcerated at Minidoka. Shimomura, *Trans-Siberian Excerpts*, Script, 1987.

33 Shimomura, "Background Information," *Trans-Siberian Excerpts*, Script, 1987.

34 This is problematic, as regardless of their citizenship and disconnect to Asia and Asian culture, Asian Americans are seen as Other and thus never seen to be as fully American as a Caucasian or European immigrant would be.

35 Roger Shimomura, *Funky Odori,* Production Script, 1987.

36 Ibid.

37 Roger Shimomura, *California Sushi,* Production Script, Introduction, 1988.

38 The model minority myth or stereotype is the perception of all Asian Americans as being more academically, economically, and socially successful than other minority groups. This misperception is harmful on many levels. For example, it exaggerates that all Asians are academically, economically, and socially successful, when there are dozens of first-generation Asian and Pacific Islander minority groups that are part of the working class; it silences and isolates less successful Asian Americans from receiving aid and pits Asian Americans against other minority groups; and it places unrealistic expectations and assumptions on Asian Americans about their abilities.

39 In 1987, through an act of the U.S. Congress, "The Stars and Stripes Forever," a composition by John Philip Sousa, became the official national march song of the United States of America.

40 Created about thirteen hundred years ago, Noh is an older, aristocratic form of Japanese theater that Kabuki was modeled after.

41 The Civil Liberties Act of 1988 granted reparations to Japanese Americans (still alive) who were unjustly incarcerated by the U.S. government during World War II. The legislation stated that government actions were not based on evidence of legitimate security reasons, but rather on "race prejudice, war hysteria, and a failure of political leadership" <https://www.congress.gov/bill/100th-congress/house-bill/442>.

42 Shimomura apologizes if his work is seen as offensive by "decent Americans," as that is not the intent of his art. Roger Shimomura, *California Sushi,* Production Script, Introduction, 1988.

43 Ibid.

44 In the late 1960s, Valeda and all segregated Greek sororities and fraternities were dismantled. The bylaws were rewritten to be inclusive of persons of non-Caucasian heritage.

45 Roger Shimomura, *California Sushi,* Production Script, Introduction,1988.

46 A partial sound bite of Haiku Rap is recorded at <https://archive.org/details/ShimomuraPerformanceMusic02>.

47 Roger Shimomura, *California Sushi,* Production Script, Introduction, 1988.

48 Ibid.

49 Ibid.

50 Ibid.

51 Ibid.

52 Ibid.

53 Ibid.

54 Ibid.

55 Ibid.

56 "Guilty by Reason of Race" was first aired on September 19, 1972.

57 Bugle was heard every morning during incarceration, reminding internees of the militaristic nature of their imprisonment. The author of the poem is unknown. The poem was translated by Dr. Kimiko Yamamoto, Japanese Language Department, University of Kansas. Dr. Yamamoto noticed a particular rhythm in the words and connected it to a famous Japanese folk melody. Shimomura, Interview with the artist, September 2, 2016.

58 "How to Tell Your Friends from the Japs," Time Magazine, Vol. XXXVIII, No. 25 (December 22, 1941), 33.

59 Homi K. Bhabha, "Of Mimicry and Man: The Ambivalence of Colonial Discourse," in *Location of Culture,* New York: Routledge, 1994, 121–131.

60 Roger Shimomura, *Campfire Diary,* Production Script, 1992.

61 Roger Shimomura, *The Last Sansei Story,* Production Script, 1993.

62 Ibid.

63 Picture brides immigrated to the United States from 1908–1924 due to the 1908 Gentleman's Agreement Act and 1924 Immigration Act that ended large-scale immigration to the United States.

64 Shimomura clarifies that the word "Sister" was an informal term his grandmother used to describe friends. Shimomura, Interview with the artist, September 26, 2016.

65 Western influence in Japan dates to the Nanban period (1543–1614) and, again, during the Meiji period (1868–1915), when trade with the West was again permitted.

66 Since most immigrants were bachelors, this was an effort to foster family bonds and aid the success of Japanese nationals.

67 Roger Shimomura, *The Last Sansei Story,* Production Script, 1993.

68 Ibid.

69 Ibid.

70 Shimomura, Interview with the artist, September 26, 2016.

71 Roger Shimomura, *The Last Sansei Story*, Production Script, 1993.

72 Shimomura added the derogatory nickname "Boy" to Dan Wildcat's name to underline the erroneous Asian cultural references all blended together in Wildcat's original song parody. "Yellow All Same" is a parody of misperception and stereotypes.

73 "Yellow All Same" was written by Dan "Boy" Wildcat.

74 Roger Shimomura, *The Last Sansei Story*, Production Script, 1993.

75 For more information see "Detroit Asian-Americans Protest Lenient Penalties for Murder," in The New York Times (April 26, 1983).

76 Roger Shimomura, *The Last Sansei Story*, Script, 1993.

77 Roger Shimomura, Interview with the artist, September 26, 2016. For more information see http://creativetime.org/projects/42nd-street-art-project-2/.

78 These periodicals provide a sampling of the reception of the 1993 Whitney Museum's Biennale and the identity politics debate stirring within the art world. <http://www.nytimes.com/1993/03/05/arts/at-the-whitney-a-biennial-with-a-social-conscience.html?pagewanted=all>, < http://nymag.com/arts/art/features/jerry-saltz-1993-art/>, < http://articles.latimes.com/1993-03-10/entertainment/ca-1335_1_art-world>.

79 Roger Shimomura, Interview with the artist, September 26, 2016.

80 A happening is a performance, event, or situation and is considered a type of performance art. It was devised as an anti-institutional art form due to its temporality and existence outside of institutional walls.

81 *Campfire Diary* toured separately for two years and was performed at twelve separate venues.

82 "Compas" is a layered rhythm and beat created with knuckles and the clapping of hands. "Palmas" refers to flamenco music and dance.

Made in the USA
Columbia, SC
10 July 2019